GOD UNDERSTANDS

*encouragement
from the
book of Daniel*

by Jeremy Mattek

Published by Straight Talk Books
P.O. Box 301, Milwaukee, WI 53201
800.661.3311 · timeofgrace.org

Copyright © 2025 Time of Grace Ministry

All rights reserved. This publication may not be copied, photocopied, reproduced, translated, or converted to any electronic or machine-readable form in whole or in part, except for brief quotations, without prior written approval from Time of Grace Ministry.

Scripture is taken from THE HOLY BIBLE, NEW INTERNATIONAL VERSION®, NIV®. Copyright © 1973, 1978, 1984, 2011 by Biblica, Inc.® Used by permission. All rights reserved worldwide.

Printed in the United States of America

ISBN: 978-1-965694-22-0

TIME OF GRACE *is a registered mark of Time of Grace Ministry.*

CONTENTS

Introduction 5

God Understands Your World: Daniel Chapter 1 9

God Understands Your Future: Daniel Chapter 2 21

God Understands Your Challenges: Daniel Chapter 3 43

God Understands Your Limits: Daniel Chapter 4 75

God Understands Your Legacy: Daniel Chapter 5 108

God Understands Your Lions: Daniel Chapter 6 143

INTRODUCTION

I was alone on the floor of my office. Before that day, I don't recall ever crumbling into the fetal position or believing I would ever find myself there. But there I was. My cheek was pressed against the floor. My tears were wetting the carpet.

I didn't try to wipe them away. I didn't have the strength. I was hurting. And hopeless. And crushed.

That's when my phone started vibrating.

It was on the floor right in front of my face. I had been using it all morning to make phone calls, and all of them had been difficult. When I finally completed the last call, the emotions I had worked so hard to hold in during every conversation could not be held in any longer. I exploded into tears and fell to the ground. I'm pretty sure I believed I would never get back up on my feet again.

I paused before looking at the caller ID. I didn't want another phone call. But I looked, and it was Dan. So I picked up.

Dan wasn't someone with whom I needed to have a difficult phone call that day, but he knew why I was making them. He was calling to see how I was doing. I couldn't have lied if I tried.

Something happened after my phone call with Dan. I got back up on my feet again. During the call, I stopped crying. Just before that, I believed it was going to be OK. I was going to be OK. How did that happen? Dan reminded me that there's a different way to look at our lives than the way we often do. We can see our lives as God does.

Always victorious.

That is what we are as we live our lives in connection with Jesus. Risen from death, he proved himself capable of overcoming any difficulty we might ever face—even the ones for which we have no answers and against which we have little, if any, strength.

In Jesus, **"we are more than conquerors through him who loved us. . . . Neither death nor life . . . neither the present nor the future . . . neither height nor depth, nor anything else in all creation, will be able to separate us from the love of God that is in Christ Jesus our Lord"** (Romans 8:37-39).

Add to that list: difficult phone calls and crumbling emotions.

Add to that list anything that discourages our fragile hearts—sickness, sadness, guilt, pain, loneliness, confusion, and loss—as we live in a world that sometimes makes it very difficult to see God. But if God is for us, the Bible asks in the book of Romans, we never need to be discouraged.

And God is for us.

"He who did not spare his own Son, but gave him up for us all—how will he not also, along with him, graciously give us all things? Who will bring any charge against those whom God has chosen?" (Romans 8:32,33).

Look at the life of Jesus. See what he gave.

Look at his death. See what he gave up. For you.

INTRODUCTION

God has chosen to love you. He has chosen to forgive you. He has chosen to make you his own. And he is not going back on those choices. He's all in.

That's what Dan helped me see. He showed me Jesus. The same Jesus I knew but whom I had a hard time seeing on account of all the difficulty that was in front of me.

I don't know if you've ever ended up on the floor of an office wetting the carpet with your tears. But I know you live in the same world I do. You live with the same type of fragile and far-too-easily-swayed heart that lives in me. I know life often feels chaotic. Whether it's the pressure of work, family struggles, health challenges, blatant opposition to your faith, or a world that seems to shift beneath your feet, it can sometimes be very difficult to believe that you're going to be OK.

That's why we all need a Dan.

And you happen to have one. Well . . . a Daniel, actually.

The Bible's book of Daniel was written in a time of exile and uncertainty. Daniel wasn't where he wanted to be. Things weren't going the way he wanted them to go. But by looking at God's great care of his life in those difficult settings, we receive a fascinating and unique reminder of God's perspective on our lives. In powerful and beautiful ways, God uses this Bible book to remind us how God knows and understands everything about us—our world and its challenges, our weaknesses and vulnerabilities. Everything.

God knows you. And he wants you to know you're going to be OK.

GOD UNDERSTANDS

I invite you to join me as we journey through the first six chapters of the book of Daniel together, allowing God to be God as he equips us for courageous Christian lives in a corrupted world.

P.S. The name of the friend who called me really is Dan. I didn't just make that up for a neat connection with the book of Daniel. ☺

P.P.S. Thank you, Dan. I'll never forget how God cared for me through you.

—Pastor Jeremy

GOD UNDERSTANDS YOUR WORLD

—

Daniel Chapter 1

GOD UNDERSTANDS

DAY 1: CULTURE MATTERS

Open Your Bible
Read Daniel 1:1–7.

On January 1, 2025, a man named Shamsud-Din Jabbar drove a rented pickup truck from Houston, Texas, to New Orleans, Louisiana. He turned his truck onto famous Bourbon Street around 3:15 A.M. and intentionally rammed through crowds of people who were celebrating the new year, killing more than a dozen of them and injuring dozens more. He then began to fire his gun at police officers who were on the scene before he himself was shot and killed by a police officer.

This is a horribly sad reminder of how unexpectedly painful life in this world can become. There are many such reminders in many different categories of life. You have likely experienced many of them.

But this reminder was also something more.

It was also a reminder that culture matters.

"Culture" is the setting in which you live. It includes not only the specific place you reside but also every voice and opinion that influences your life and the choices you make within it.

The man who drove that truck into New Orleans and caused so much pain had served for years in the US military. As a member of the US military, he was someone who had promised he would use his life only and always to defend the lives of others. From what we've learned about this man, he took that promise seriously. His personal culture—the one in which he lived, the one he communicated to others through his words and actions—was one of loving sacrifice and service. He helped others. He saved lives. He defended the innocent.

So how did he become someone so different?

He was influenced by another voice that exists in this world (there are many). One that promotes violence. One that promises to murder the innocent if that's what it takes to get people to pay attention to what that voice is saying. At first, no doubt, he just listened. He maybe even pushed back a bit since this new voice was saying things that were so contrary to what he had heard and believed previously. But over time as he kept listening, this new voice became the primary influencer of his culture.

His culture changed. And as a result, so did he.

Culture matters.

That's what the Babylonians were counting on as they brought Daniel and many of his contemporaries to live among them.

Daniel had lived and grown up in Judah. But in 605 B.C.—the third year of the reign of Jehoiakim king of Judah—the Babylonians, who had become a dominant world power, invaded Judah and took many of its citizens captive to Babylon. This was the first of three times over the next 20 years the Babylonians would do this to the people of Judah.

The Babylonians didn't take everyone, and they didn't take just anyone. They only took the best—the smartest, the most intelligent, the strongest, and the most capable. They took those who, if they were to live willingly as citizens of Babylon, would make this strong world power even stronger. This is why the Babylonians didn't put these "prisoners" in prisons. In addition to receiving new Babylonian names, they were given important jobs and prominent positions in their new home. They were trained in the Babylonian language, literature, and customs. This wasn't just education. It was indoctrination.

The Babylonians knew that at first their newest residents would miss their homes and families in Judah. But eventually as time went on and the people and voices of Babylon became more and more familiar to them, they would adjust to and maybe even embrace their new culture and serve it well. The Babylonians believed that at some point, Babylon would feel like home and the exiles would happily treat it as such.

Culture matters. There are many of them—people, ideas, and ideologies that want your allegiance, love, and trust. Wherever you are in the world, you are regularly bombarded with voices that want to influence your culture and, as a result, your actions. These voices come through your television and books, through the countless apps on your phone, from the people at your job or school, and even from the people in your home.

You and I live in a culture where advertisers want us to buy their stuff; politicians want our votes; social media influencers want our time, attention, and adoration. Meanwhile their fame and wealth can influence how we spend our time and use our God-given talents. It's a culture where every relationship, intentionally or accidentally, is a voice of influence—not all bad, much of it good. Navigating it all in a way that makes us feel as if life isn't getting the best of us can be a difficult task. It's overwhelming for many and impossible for some.

This is why Christians must return regularly to the cross of Jesus. There we find a culture of unconditional love. There we find a declaration of forgiveness for every misstep and sin. There we find security in God's attention to our deepest needs. There we hear someone bigger than us promising always to use his bigness for our benefit. There we see God never giving up on us. Ever.

You know, there aren't many cultures in the world where all of that is freely offered, which is why we must never remove ourselves or allow ourselves to be moved from the culture of our God's love for us in Jesus. That is our one, always-reliable place of safety. But finding it has always been more challenging than we would like.

It was for Daniel too. We see his reality in the second verse of chapter 1. In that verse, Nebuchadnezzar, the ruler of Babylon, took what had been dedicated to the true God in the temple in Jerusalem and put those things in the treasure house of his own god. By that action, Nebuchadnezzar was saying that Jerusalem's God (Daniel's God, our God, the God of the Bible) was no match for him—his power, his will, his intentions, or the culture he wanted to create. History would prove him wrong, of course.

Over the course of the book of Daniel, Daniel and his friends will show us that living in a different place and a difficult culture doesn't mean we are ever living or have to live without the God who understands the cultural challenges we face and wants us to know he is here to face them with us.

Review Daniel 1:1-7.

Real Life

Sarah landed her dream job at a prestigious firm, but the corporate culture was anything but welcoming to her Christian values. From office gossip to ethical compromises, she often felt like an outsider. One day, her supervisor mocked her faith in a meeting. Everyone noticed. She felt humiliated.

1. What options do you think Sarah had at that point?

2. What course of action do you think would have made the most positive impression on her coworkers?

Questions

1. What voices have the most influence on your personal culture currently?

   HINT: If you're a social media user, your phone can likely give you a detailed report on the exact number of minutes you spend on each platform every day. Check this without feeling the need to condemn yourself or anyone else. Remember that **"there is now no condemnation for those who are in Christ Jesus"** (Romans 8:1). Use this as an opportunity to learn and grow.

   If you're not a social media user, think about keeping it that way. ☺ Look instead at your primary sources of news and information (books, magazines, talk shows, television networks, neighbors, etc.).

2. What cultures do you see in the world that are contrary to a God-pleasing culture?

3. What cultures in the world do you believe are most dangerous for Christians and their ability to live God-pleasing lives?

4. What about the culture of Jesus do you appreciate the most? Think of some practical ways you can "live" there a bit more regularly.

DAY 2: COURAGE MATTERS

Open Your Bible
Read Daniel 1:8-21.

I don't remember ever liking the taste of squash. Nor do I remember when I first made that evaluation. In truth, I don't think I ever gave it a fair shot. I think I just decided it was a vegetable I wasn't going to eat. I didn't want to say that to the loving people who were trying to feed me healthy food that would help me grow in healthy ways. So I didn't.

As far as I can remember, my first experience with squash was when I was very young—two or three years old maybe. I was small enough that I still needed a booster seat to eat at the "big" table with the rest of the family. That booster seat happened to have a nice little compartment underneath it. It opened from the front. It was, I thought, the ideal place to hide my squash.

When a helping of squash was placed on my plate, I would scoop it up with my spoon and bring the spoon to my open mouth. But instead of putting the spoon into my open mouth, I would close my mouth just before the spoon arrived and start "chewing" (not that I was actually chewing anything; there was nothing in my mouth) as I diverted the spoon full of squash to the little compartment underneath my booster seat. I quickly unloaded the squash from my spoon before bringing the empty spoon back to the table in full view of anyone who may or may not have cared to wonder if I was eating my veggies.

I know. Brilliant. ☺

Actually, it wasn't. It took me quite a while to realize that the little compartment under the booster seat didn't have a bottom. So when someone cleaned up after dinner and removed my booster seat from the chair, my discarded pile of squash was right there. Most often, it was my mom who found that pile. She knew how I felt about my veggies. And like a good mom, she kept giving them to me.

I don't know how Daniel felt about eating squash, but there was more at stake in his veggie story in chapter 1 than whether or not he was getting his daily dose of vitamins.

King Nebuchadnezzar presented his employees with the richest foods and the finest wines, expecting they would enjoy them. That sounds generous! What's wrong with that?

The problem was that the food and wine enjoyed regularly by the king and those around him had been dedicated to their god—who was not at all the same God Daniel worshiped. In Babylon, eating and drinking was an act of allegiance to their false god. Daniel knew that if he participated, he would give the impression to everyone there that he believed in their god. And his conscience couldn't live with that.

Taking a stand on this issue required something very

important. It required courage. Nebuchadnezzar had a reputation for very quickly dishing out the worst types of punishments to anyone who disobeyed him in any way, and Daniel had no way of predicting what would happen if he turned down food offered by the king. But he couldn't do nothing, so he came up with a plan.

Daniel had gained the respect of the king's chief official and knew that official would hear him out without outing him. Daniel suggested a plan, a ten-day trial. For ten days, Daniel and his friends would eat only vegetables and drink only water. After the ten days, the official would evaluate them and take whatever action he thought would be best based on his evaluation of their strength and job performance over those ten days. Daniel promised the official that he wouldn't be disappointed, and Daniel was right.

At the end of ten days, Daniel and his friends were dramatically healthier and did their jobs significantly better than their peers who ate the king's diet. The king noticed. He not only commended them; he promoted them.

How did that happen? It wasn't because of the veggies they ate. It was the God whose love and care were the basis for their courage.

God not only blessed their bodies with the new diet; he also equipped them to do their jobs better than anyone else could by giving them increased knowledge and understanding. God had their backs, just as he has yours. And you don't need to go through a ten-day test of veggie eating to know it. You only need to remember that God himself also needed courage.

It took courage to leave heaven and put on human flesh knowing that one day nails would be driven through him. It took courage to keep going when the people who should have loved him didn't. It took courage to hang on a cross designed for criminals though he was innocent. It took courage to pay the price that would result in all your sins being forgiven.

Jesus was courageous so that you can live with the comfort that comes from knowing that God will always have your back. Always. Especially when your faith is challenged.

You might sometimes wonder why God allows you to be in positions where your faith isn't supported. Daniel's veggie story reminds you and me of one possible reason. God wanted Daniel and his friends to be in a place where they could help people who did not know God or see God so these people could see God's power, how he cares for his people, and the reason for Daniel's courage.

In a world as broken as ours is, every person needs courage. Every person needs to see God. They may never find him without first seeing you and your faith-filled courage. Your courage matters.

Review Daniel 1:8-21.

Real Life

A young engineer named David discovered his company was cutting corners on safety to save costs. When he voiced his concerns, he faced threats of demotion, and some of his coworkers began to avoid him. Sometimes they intentionally made his job more difficult. David knew that many in the company were also Christians. They didn't make his job more difficult, but they didn't voice their support for him openly either.

1. What options do you think David had at that point?

2. What course of action do you believe would most inspire his fellow Christians and also help the non-Christians see the heart of Jesus most clearly?

Questions

1. Explain: Courage is not the absence of fear but the presence of faith.

2. Does it take more courage to live your faith when you're surrounded by people who don't share your faith or when you're all by yourself faced with a strong temptation? Explain your answer.

3. What promise from God or biblical account inspires you to be courageous?

GOD UNDERSTANDS YOUR FUTURE

—

Daniel Chapter 2

DAY 3: AN IMPOSSIBLE TASK

Open Your Bible
Read Daniel 2:1–18.

I had a dream recently. Can you tell me what it was? I'll wait . . .

I won't tell you any details about the dream. I will only tell you it was very troubling to me. My heart was racing when I woke up, and I tried to convince myself that it was only a dream—that it wasn't real and didn't mean anything. That's all the info I'm going to give you though. Now tell me the details of my dream, and also explain it. What was it saying about my life. Please don't mess this up. It's important.

I'm still waiting . . .

I think you know I would have to wait for quite a while. After all, how would you know that in my dream I was standing near someone I care about deeply in a location where a man with a bomb strapped to himself was also standing? You couldn't know the details. Here's more: The bomb must have gone off because the scene suddenly changed to someone I love hearing the news that two people (me and the person with me) had been injured in an explosion and that one was in critical condition. The report didn't say who was in critical condition. But then in a strange, only-in-a-dream kind of way, I had to make a decision in that moment that would dictate the past—and also the future. I had to choose who had been critically injured while somehow knowing that the person I chose would not make it. That person would die while the other person would live. That was the dream.

Now that I've shared those details with you, you might try to tell me what you think the dream means, if it means anything (so far, nothing in my reality has come anywhere close to matching the details of this dream—so it's possible that it really was just a dream). But for me to ask you to tell me all those details—even though you didn't dream my dream nor were you in my dream—well, I think you might see that as an unreasonable and impossible request.

Yet that's the request that King Nebuchadnezzar made of his advisors. Nebuchadnezzar had a troubling dream. Discovering the meaning of his dream was incredibly important to him. He didn't want anyone to guess at its meaning, so he didn't even share the details of the dream with anyone. He demanded that his advisors tell him both the details of the dream and its correct meaning—with the promise that they would be killed immediately if they didn't do both.

Yes, it was an unreasonable demand. But as one of the king's advisors, it was still Daniel's reality. His future was unknown, as so much of it always is.

Nebuchadnezzar was as uncertain about the meaning of his dream as we are about the future. Will someone you love get cancer? Will you? Is the company for which you work going to be here in five years? How about the people you love and rely on the most? Will they be here? Will you get married? Will you have children? Will they love you? Will you love you? Will you carry deep regrets on your heart when you look back on your life?

Since there are so many important things about the future that we do not know, it's important to remember one truth about the future we do know: **"My Father's house has many rooms,"** Jesus said. **"I am going there to prepare a place for you"** (John 14:2).

What kind of place? One where God **"will wipe every tear from their eyes. There will be no more death or mourning or crying or pain"** (Revelation 21:4). Our eventual future is guaranteed to be completely unlike our present. That's what Jesus guaranteed for you and me.

"He saved us, not because of righteous things we had done, but because of his mercy" (Titus 3:5). Don't miss the significance of the word "righteous" in this verse. That word means "perfect," "the best," "the highest possible quality." And your future with God does *not* at all depend on that word accurately describing you.

In other words, your future doesn't depend on how purely you've lived, on how faithful you have or haven't been. It doesn't depend on what percentage of the time you have overcome temptations to sin successfully. It doesn't depend on your ability to know or interpret dreams. It doesn't depend on you at all.

It depends entirely on Jesus' choice to show you mercy, which is exactly what he did when he left heaven knowing exactly what was waiting for him in the future. What was waiting was a cross on which he suffered a punishment for sins that were not his. They were yours and mine—and as a result, we are forgiven. You are forgiven.

This is why the Bible assures us that **"neither the present nor the future, nor any powers, neither height nor depth, nor anything else in all creation, will be able to separate us from the love of God that is in Christ Jesus"** (Romans 8:38,39). That's God's promise to you. He will make sure it is fulfilled.

Maybe that's why Daniel stepped into this impossible dream-interpreting situation with such confidence. Even if Nebuchadnezzar took Daniel's life, Daniel was never going to lose his God or his future.

The knowledge of his future had an impact on his present, just as it should for you. If nothing can separate you from the love of God, that not only means God will love you in the future. It means he is loving you right now and always in a way that keeps you close to him.

Daniel saw that in a very special way that day. I'll talk more about that in the upcoming sections. But for now, rest your soul in the certainty that the God who knows the future knows how impossible your life can often be. He will not fail to show you mercy.

Review Daniel 2:1-18.

Real Life

Maria, a single mother, lost her job unexpectedly. Bills piled up, and fear of the future consumed her. She felt helpless, so she prayed to God.

1. For what would you pray first if you were in Maria's situation?

2. Can you think of someone in your life who is currently fearful of the future? What's one truth from the book of Daniel you might use to encourage them? Think of a way to reach out to them and share that truth with them.

Questions

1. Which do you find most comforting today (explain your answer)?
   - That God knows the future
   - That God is with you in the present
   - That God has forgiven your past.

2. Write down something about the future that troubles you. Tell God about it. Explain to him why it troubles you. Then ask God to deal with the situation on your behalf, remembering his promise to treat you with mercy and love.

DAY 4: WHO GOD REALLY IS

Open Your Bible
Read Daniel 2:19–23.

I remember some years ago hearing big news out of a country in southern Africa called Botswana. Someone had discovered what was at the time the second-largest diamond ever found. It was 1,111 carats. To put that in some perspective, a 100-carat diamond had recently been sold at an auction in New York for $22.1 million. So the Botswana diamond was a valuable diamond!

Though no one had seen this diamond before its recent discovery, it had been in existence for quite a while—hidden in the ground somewhere, undiscovered, yet just as valuable as any discovered or yet undiscovered 1,111-carat diamond.

Daniel reminds us that something similar is true about our God. Whether or not people realize it, he's been around for quite a while. In fact, he's actually been around for much longer than any diamond. He's been here for ever and ever.

That's what Daniel reminded himself of in the prayer he offered to God after God had revealed to Daniel not only the meaning of King Nebuchadnezzar's dream but also the contents of the dream itself. He reminded himself of the truth that God was around long before the king was and that he'll be around long after the king and Daniel would both be gone.

The king who acted like he owned Daniel's life could only do so much. After God revealed the dream and its meaning to Daniel, that's a truth Daniel found comfort in. But it wasn't the only truth.

When we think of prayer, we often picture ourselves asking God for something. That's not wrong at all. Jesus himself commands us to pray and invites us to **"ask"** with the promise that **"it will be given to you"** (Matthew 7:7). But Daniel shows us here that we can use our prayers for another purpose. The purpose of remembering who our God is.

As you read through Daniel's prayer, did you notice that Daniel never actually asked for *anything*. Rather, his prayer is a compilation of different characteristics of God. Consider those characteristics and what they say about your God:

"Wisdom and power are his."—God is smarter than you and can do things you never could. There's no situation he doesn't understand. Nothing is impossible for him—not even coming back from death to assure you that his redemption plan was complete, that one day you will rise just as he did, and that nothing, not even his own death, is going to stop him from being with you and for you.

"He changes times and seasons."—God's power isn't bound by seasons or calendars or deadlines. He created seasons and time. He can change them when needed just as he once did when he made the sun stand still to help his people in battle (Joshua 10).

"He deposes kings and raises up others."—Every ruler in the history of our planet has always been accountable to God, knowingly or not, and God has used their time in power to serve his good purpose whether or not they wanted him to. God is the King of kings.

"He gives wisdom to the wise and knowledge to the discerning. He reveals deep and hidden things."—God shares with you important information you need for your life, information you could never find on your own, the most important piece of which is knowledge of Jesus as your Savior. Jesus secured your future with God by his sacrifice on a cross. You live by faith in God's promises, not by faith in your ability to figure life out successfully.

"He knows what lies in darkness."—No one's sin is invisible to God; no one can hide anything from him. Additionally, he knows why worry, fear, and guilt live in the darkest places of your heart. He knows how to find them, and . . .

"Light dwells with him."— . . . he knows how to lead you to a place of peace. As a light reveals the path ahead of you, God has revealed his love for you in Jesus. It's a love that has no conditions and has declared you forgiven of every sin. God keeps you close to that love with the guidance he gives in his Word.

Daniel called God the *"God of my ancestors."*—Your God isn't the new shiny thing in the world. He has a history of helping his people. People you know. People just like you.

Finally, Daniel praised God for answering his particular prayers. He asked God for the impossible—for detailed knowledge of someone else's dream and for the correct interpretation of that dream. **"You have given me wisdom and power, you have made known to me what we asked of you, you have made known to us the dream of the king"** (2:23).

And then Daniel's prayer was done. He never asked for anything in this prayer, but he still accomplished something so significant. He remembered who God is—and how incredibly comforting God's identity is for all of us.

But not everyone has discovered that. Like the Botswana diamond that was undiscovered for so many years, God's identity, his love for us in Jesus, and how he graciously uses all he is for our benefit remains undiscovered by so many in our world.

There are many people living their lives as if God's not real. Even those who know him can become so easily blinded by the troubles of life or by the reality of their own failures that they easily forget God's promise to care for them always and forever.

This is why Daniel's prayer is such a great model for you today. It helps you remember who God really is—and how safe you always are with him.

Review Daniel 2:19-23.

Real Life

James had been praying to God for healing after a serious illness. For a long time, it seemed God wasn't listening to his prayer. His condition, in fact, only got worse. Then a friend suggested to James that it seemed he was telling God what to do rather than trusting God to do what God knew was best. He reminded James of the promise in Romans 8:28 that God will work all things out for the good of those who love him. James' next prayer was different. He thanked God for being merciful and told God he would be content with whatever God decided to do with his illness. A week later, James was no longer sick, and the doctors didn't have an explanation for it.

1. Why do you think God decided to deal with James in this way—waiting until his prayer changed before healing him?

2. Explain why you think James changed his prayer.

Questions

1. Go through the list of what Daniel said about God in his prayer along with their explanations. Identify your favorite characteristic of God from that list. Explain why you chose what you did.

2. Can you think of any other characteristics of God revealed in the Bible that are particularly comforting to you? How can you better keep those characteristics on your mind as you go through each day?

DAY 5: ONLY GOD CAN

Open Your Bible
Read Daniel 2:24-28.

Aaron, who was in his 20s, had been color-blind for his entire life. There were certain colors he simply could not see. Most things looked black and white.

For his birthday, his parents bought him glasses with special lenses that were supposed to help a color-blind person see all the colors. Aaron decided to put the glasses on for the first time while looking at a sunset. The glasses worked. Suddenly Aaron could see all the beautiful colors he had never seen previously.

Do you know how Aaron reacted?

When Aaron put on his special glasses and looked at the beautiful sunset, his lips started quivering. He started shaking. He started crying. He couldn't say anything. Everyone could tell that he had seen something amazing. The special glasses did something amazing for Aaron.

God did something amazing for Daniel. He revealed to Daniel not only the correct meaning of Nebuchadnezzar's troubling dream but also the details of the dream itself—which Nebuchadnezzar had not shared with Daniel or anyone else. God did that. And Daniel wanted everyone to know it was *God* who did it—and that was risky.

Nebuchadnezzar seems to have been a quick-tempered king. One moment he might invite you to share a generous feast of the finest foods around his table. The next moment, with no explanation, he might sentence you to death and kick your dog while he's at it.

So when the king asked Daniel, "Are you able to tell me what I saw in my dream and interpret it?" and the first word out of Daniel's mouth was "No," Daniel was maybe hoping the king wouldn't fly off the handle immediately. But Daniel was certainly determined to give credit where credit was due. He quickly explained that God is the one who "reveals mysteries." Daniel didn't know the dream and its meaning. Only God did. And if only God did, that meant that Daniel didn't.

It wouldn't have been a lie for Daniel to answer the king's question by saying, "Yes! I am able to tell you what was in your dream. And yes! I am also able to tell you what it means." After all, he was just about to prove that was true by correctly telling Nebuchadnezzar both the dream and its meaning. Very few would have blamed Daniel for carefully choosing to say it that way in front of the quick-tempered king in order to give himself the best possible chance of living.

But in Daniel's actual choice of words, we see a humble acknowledgment of something Jesus once said to his disciples: **"Apart from me you can do nothing"** (John 15:5). And Jesus meant *nothing*.

You would not exist if God had not chosen to create you.

You can't breathe without God's permission. You would have no knowledge of anything at all if God did not give it to you—and no ability to do anything with it if God didn't provide you with a brain that can process and store remarkable amounts of information. You would have no way to anticipate a good future if God had not done everything to prepare it for you. And he has.

Just like Aaron used his special glasses to look at a beautiful sunrise and saw something amazing, so also your eyes will one day see something beautiful. On the day the sun finally sets on this earth, you will see Jesus coming to take you home. He's the One who was whipped and pierced for your benefit, who has the scars to prove his love for you, who carried the heavy weight of your sins for you because he knew you couldn't handle it. You know it will happen because Jesus did all that was necessary to make it happen. **"For it is by grace you have been saved, through faith—and this is not from yourselves, it is the gift of God—not by works, so that no one can boast"** (Ephesians 2:8,9).

Maybe no one would blame Daniel for boasting. But Daniel knew he had no reason to do such a thing. Neither do you.

It seems that in the world today, in order to get anywhere, you need to make yourself look as good as you possibly can. It's why people only share the positive things about their lives on social media—so no one knows their struggles or weaknesses. It's why people most often say, "I'm fine" when someone asks them how they're doing—even if they're not. They want to look competent and capable. It's why so much effort goes into producing the perfect résumé and why kids (and their parents) stress out so much about test scores and GPAs. The world expects you to do something, but God just wants your soul to rest in all he's done so perfectly, so completely, and so graciously for your benefit.

Daniel's soul was obviously at rest that day. Daniel only needed to be who Daniel already was. He didn't need to prove anything. Neither do you.

By the work of Jesus, you belong to God. You belong to GOD. That's enough. You're enough.

Review Daniel 2:24-28.

Real Life

Emma, a high school senior, had just received a rejection letter from her preferred college. Her parents told her how disappointed they were in her and said she should have worked harder. She checked her social media and soon saw a number of her classmates celebrating their acceptance into their preferred colleges.

1. What message from this chapter might you share with Emma to encourage her?

2. How would Jesus answer the question, "Who is Emma?"

Questions

1. In what areas of your life are you feeling pressure to prove something about yourself?

2. How does this part of Daniel help you better live in peace rather than pressure?

3. Daniel seemed to have a good understanding of who he was *to God*. That gave him peace to do the best job he could of being himself. Which of the following truths about who you are because of Jesus means the most to you right now:

- You are loved by God.
- You are forgiven of every sin.
- You are wonderfully made by God, his work of art, and unique compared to every other person who has ever lived.
- You are eternally victorious.

DAY 6: YOU HAVE A ROCK

Open Your Bible
Read Daniel 2:28-49.

The first dream I remember having turned out to be pretty accurate. I don't recall my exact age. I know I was under the age of 5. In my dream, I was running through the house because I was being chased by spiders, and not just your normal, everyday spiders. These spiders were GIANT! Their skinny legs and ugly torsos filled the room from floor to ceiling. And they were chasing me.

I remember running through the house as quickly as my little legs could carry me. I darted into my bedroom and went under the bed as the giant spiders followed and extended their ugly skinny legs toward me and . . . I woke up. That was the end of the dream.

Many decades later, I still have a pretty severe dislike of spiders. Did the dream cause that dislike, or did it reveal something that was already there and was already going to happen? I don't know.

But we do know that Nebuchadnezzar's dream wasn't just a dream. It was a prediction of what was going to happen in the future. Looking back now, many centuries later, we can determine with pretty good accuracy what it all meant.

In his dream was a statue of a person. Different parts of that person's body were made of different materials, and each of those parts/materials represented a nation that either was currently or would be eventually a dominant world power.

Here's a summary of those parts and what world powers they represented:

Head/gold: Babylonians (Nebuchadnezzar's kingdom)

Chest and arms/silver: Medes and Persians

Belly and thighs/bronze: Greece

Legs and feet/iron and clay: Rome

By this dream, God was telling Nebuchadnezzar what God knew about the future. God knew not only which kingdoms (some of which didn't exist at the time) would become dominant on the world stage, but he also knew certain characteristics of them—how their power would compare to Babylon's, whether there would be peace or division within their governments, etc.

But there's one important aspect of this dream and its meaning that wouldn't have been lost on Nebuchadnezzar: His kingdom was temporary. It was one day going to come to an end. The God who gave him his power was one day going to take it away.

Life gives us all reminders of the same thing. We get a phone call letting us know that someone we love has died. We lose our job. The economy tanks, destroying our net worth. A marriage falls apart. A family is divided. We lose our resolve to keep trying after yet another failure. Our bodies become weak with age. They don't recover as quickly as they once did. Or at all.

What was true for Nebuchadnezzar—for all those nations, really (none of them exist today, not in the same dominant world power kind of way)—is also true for us: Our "kingdoms," the lives we work so hard to build for ourselves, are temporary.

But one thing isn't temporary.

In Nebuchadnezzar's dream, there was also a rock, one made **"not by human hands,"** that destroyed the entire statue and **"became a huge mountain and filled the whole earth."** This rock was more significant and powerful than any of the nations. This rock did not come from a worldly kingdom. This rock impacts the whole world. **"That rock was Christ,"** we read in 1 Corinthians 10:4. Here the apostle Paul wasn't talking specifically about Nebuchadnezzar's dream. He was talking about what gives us a good life and eternity, reminding us of the same thing God wanted to teach Nebuchadnezzar— that there is something reliable on which we can establish our fragile lives. There is solid ground on which our shaky souls can stand. There is something dependable we can put our hope in when our personal kingdoms are falling, failing, and dying.

It is the Savior standing alive outside of the grave he

was buried in after he died. The Savior who died only because he knew just how desperately our shaky, sinful lives need a reliable foundation of love, forgiveness, and grace that will never fail even if we do, even if we die.

"If Christ has not been raised, your faith is futile; you are still in your sins. But Christ has indeed been raised from the dead" (1 Corinthians 15:17,20). So your faith is not worthless. You have been freed from any connection to your sins.

Since those truths are based on the perfectly reliable work of Jesus and not in any way on you, your work, your effort, your merit, or the quality of any kingdom you might try to build over the course of your life . . . you are now and always will be a citizen of the only kingdom that lasts forever. You last forever, because you have a rock.

> *I build on this foundation: that Jesus and his blood*
> *alone are my salvation, my true, eternal good.*
> *Without him all that pleases is valueless on earth;*
> *the gifts I have from Jesus alone have priceless worth.*

(Paul Gerhardt, "If God Himself Be for Me," stanza 3, text is public domain.)

Review Daniel 2:28-49.

Real Life

Samantha and John were married for just a few months when a natural disaster wiped out their home. It wasn't covered by insurance (to their surprise) and destroyed them financially. That's also when Samantha's mother died unexpectedly.

1. What realities from Nebuchadnezzar's dream might you share with Samantha and John to comfort them?

2. Have you ever been in a situation similar to Samantha and John? If so, try to recall something someone else did or said that helped you during that time. Look for an opportunity to provide that same type of help to someone who may need it.

Questions

1. What temporary "kingdoms" do you see people investing themselves in to an unhealthy degree in today's world?

2. This section of the book of Daniel can provide comfort to anyone who is worried about particular political rulers—comfort that God is always in control no matter who holds any particular position of earthly power. Why do you think people can become so easily discouraged, fearful, or angered by politics?

What's one truth about God and his involvement in history you can be ready to share with the next person you meet who is overly discouraged, fearful, or angry because of politics in general or because of a particular political ruler?

3. Think of one promise God gives in the Bible that makes you glad because of its reliability.

GOD UNDERSTANDS YOUR CHALLENGES

—

Daniel Chapter 3

DAY 7: YOU'LL BE SURPRISED

Open Your Bible
Read Daniel 3:1–6.

Titan is the name of a ten-year-old English Mastiff dog, and he was having a bad day. He got into a fight with a skunk. As a result, he was banned to the backyard. His family was gone for the day, and then it started raining. So Titan looked for shelter and hopped into the family golf cart, not knowing that it had not been turned off properly the last time someone was driving it, which is why when Titan's paw hit the gas pedal, the cart started moving and didn't stop until it crashed into his owner's truck and ran over a kiddie pool.

While that kiddie pool never held water again, the truck was easily fixed, and Titan walked away entirely unscathed, which is good news because often when you take a ride through life you weren't expecting—and one that gives you very little control over where you're going—you're not always so confident you're going to be OK.

Surprising rides through life aren't a new thing. Quite possibly the most famous trio in the Bible took one of those too, and it was even more difficult, dangerous, and surprising than the one Titan found himself on.

I don't believe Shadrach, Meshach, and Abednego knew their faith was going to be tested that day. They knew a statue had been built. They knew it was going to be dedicated, and they were planning to attend the dedication. There was nothing wrong with that. It would be like you attending the dedication of the Lincoln Memorial in Washington D.C.

This was a significant event for the nation of Babylon. Many of their friends and peers had invested a great deal of time, energy, effort, and talent into building the statue. By their presence at the dedication, they would be supporting their friends and their nation (which is exactly what God commanded them to do in Jeremiah chapter 29).

However, as they were there participating in the dedication, enjoying a nice day alongside their fellow citizens, there came an announcement they were not expecting: **"Fall down and worship the image"** (verse 5). They were to treat it as their god, and anyone who didn't would get an all-expenses-paid trip to a fiery furnace.

Suddenly, the three men were in a moment of unexpected crisis, and whatever they chose to do next would send a clear message. If they did as they were told, they violated their faith and their God, but they got to keep living. But if they stayed on their feet and refused to worship the image, they would reveal themselves as followers of a different God and find themselves living their last day of earthly existence—but not before they suffered the greatest physical pain they would ever experience as they smelled their own flesh burning into a pile of ashes.

I don't think they ever imagined being in such a serious test of faith. They were surprised, just as we often are. Such as when a marriage between two Christians becomes incredibly hostile and divisive and the words spoken to you by your spouse are regularly, entirely, and heart piercingly non-Christian.

Or when you're pressured at work to fudge the numbers intentionally so the report to the stockholders doesn't appear as bad as it really is.

Or when your government arrests your son and keeps him in prison for months because they want to pressure you to stop telling your clients about Jesus (true story).

Or when your good friends seem to be really happy about the wrong thing they're about to do and assure you they'll be incredibly disappointed if you don't do it too.

Or when a sin that has never tempted you previously seems to take over your heart entirely.

You and I often don't expect these types of difficult situations. They surprise us, but they shouldn't. That's what Jesus told his disciples: **"If they persecuted me, they will persecute you also"** (John 15:20). And persecute him they did. They slapped Jesus in the face while he stood there and took it. They pounded nails through Jesus' hands and feet while he calmly allowed it to happen. They spit on him and made fun of him while Jesus begged God, out loud, to forgive them. I bet that surprised them. Why would he not fight back? Why would he not complain? Why would he choose to forgive those who were hurting him? Because God promises to love us no matter what it costs him, and he doesn't want anyone to be surprised by that. He wants us to expect it.

That's why Shadrach, Meshach, and Abednego made the decision they did that day. They may not have been expecting that particular challenge of faith, just as you likely will be surprised or have already been surprised by the level of hostility that can be directed at those who identify by the title Christian. But they had learned to expect that God would not fail to love them—far better and more faithfully than this world can—when they walk with him.

We'll see that play out in the lives of these three men as we continue through Daniel chapter 3, but know that the world sees it play out in you too. You live in the same world as these three men—different nations, different times, different challenges, different surprises—but never without the same need for a God who will not fail to love you well whenever and in whatever way you are surprised by the challenges you face.

Earlier on the night when Jesus told his disciples to expect challenges of faith, he also said this to them: **"As the Father has loved me, so have I loved you"** (John 15:9).

Picture Jesus saying just those last three words to you.

"*I loved you.*"

"I loved *you.*"

The very next day, he loved you with his whole life. He loved you until death.

He did love you.

He does love you.

He will love you.

Review Daniel 3:1-6.

Real Life

Rebecca, a nurse in a large hospital, was told to carry out a procedure quickly that went against her Christian faith. When she politely refused, her superior promised to terminate her job immediately if she refused again.

1. What options did Rebecca have in that moment?

2. How would you have used the account of Shadrach, Meshach, and Abednego to help guide her?

Questions

1. Have you ever been surprised by a challenge to your faith? If so, what was it?

2. Where do you find it easiest to live your faith? Where do you currently find it most difficult?

3. Who in the Bible do you think had the most difficult challenge of faith?

GOD UNDERSTANDS YOUR CHALLENGES

DAY 8: STAND UP AND STAND OUT

Open Your Bible
Read Daniel 3:7-12.

My four brothers and I got together some years ago for a few days in Arizona. One day we were on our way out of the restaurant where we had eaten lunch when I saw a bowl of candy near the entrance. It looked like the type of bowl that many restaurants place near the entrance—one that holds a pleasant after-dinner mint for those who have just finished eating and the type I typically enjoy.

I didn't want to delay our group unnecessarily, so I moved quickly toward the bowl and turned my body toward the candy to grab a piece when—BAM!!—I ran right into the piece of glass that was between me and the bowl. I didn't see the glass (it had apparently been cleaned very well, or maybe I was just so locked in on the candy that I didn't care to look).

Thankfully, the glass didn't break. But my collision with it made a loud enough noise that it got the attention of everyone in the restaurant. Every conversation stopped immediately, and every head turned in my direction. There was no hiding from my embarrassing moment. I walked away as quickly as I could without saying anything—while my brothers couldn't stop laughing.

And no, I never got the candy.

I'm telling you that story because something similar—every eye being laser-focused on one place—is what I picture happening with Shadrach, Meshach, and Abednego when they remained standing while everyone else around them knelt to the ground to worship the image King Nebuchadnezzar had constructed.

The crowd surrounding these three men was immensely larger than the crowd in that restaurant. Multiple nations had been invited to this dedication event. We're told that **"peoples of every language"** were there and that all **"fell down and worshiped the image of gold that King Nebuchadnezzar had set up"** (verse 7). Except for the three men who remained standing. They weren't hiding in the crowd. They didn't blend in. They were different. They stood out. As uncomfortable as that may have been, we know why they did it, and so did the people of Babylon.

The group that reported their disobedience to King Nebuchadnezzar (a group of royal astrologers; they were likely coworkers of Shadrach, Meshach, and Abednego) knew Shadrach, Meshach, and Abednego worshiped the God of the Jews. That's how they were described when their disobedience to the king was reported: **"Some astrologers came forward and denounced the Jews"** (verse 8).

But now those astrologers knew something else about

them. They knew Shadrach, Meshach, and Abednego weren't going to worship anything or anyone else, no matter what it might cost them.

Sometimes standing up for God does cost something. John the Baptist stood up for God against Herod and was beheaded. Peter and John stood up for God and were arrested. So was the apostle Paul, multiple times. Additionally, in Paul's own words: **"I was beaten with rods . . . pelted with stones"** (2 Corinthians 11:25). All because he stood up for God.

Ten of Jesus' twelve disciples stood up for God and had their lives taken from them as a result. His disciple John wasn't killed for his faith but was arrested on account of it and exiled to a remote island prison, where he lived out his last days alone.

Stephen stood up for God and was killed by people throwing large stones at him. It's that account in the book of Acts that helps us answer an important question about all these disciples standing up for God: *What was God doing while all these disciples stood up for him, risking their lives and even being killed on account of it?*

In Acts chapter 7, Stephen not only stood up for God; he educated his enemies about God, sharing the history of God's activity from the Old Testament up until the present. He ended his speech by telling his audience, **"You have betrayed and murdered him"** (Acts 7:52). In putting Jesus on a cross and killing him, they were guilty of murdering God.

They didn't exactly receive that message well: **"When the members of the Sanhedrin heard this, they were** furious and gnashed their teeth at him. . . . **They covered their ears and, yelling at the top of their voices, they all rushed at him, dragged him out of the city and began to stone him"** (Acts 7:54,57,58).

In the middle of that, Stephen saw something. He **"looked up to heaven and saw the glory of God, and Jesus standing at the right hand of God"** (Acts 7:55). As Stephen was standing up for God, Jesus was standing up for Stephen. Just as Jesus does for you anytime you stand up for your faith.

You might do that publicly when people see you going against the crowd, when your coworkers witness your refusal to cross a line, when your family sees you wake up for church on Sunday morning after getting home from work only two hours earlier.

You can stand up for Jesus when you are alone too. When it's just you and a guilty conscience, you stand on God's promise that you're forgiven (Romans 8:1). When your child gets sick, you stand on God's assurance that he will provide all that they need (2 Corinthians 9:8). When life is really hard, you stand on God's promise to hear your every prayer and answer each one (Psalm 50:15). You stand up for Jesus when you feel really alone yet with the very little strength you have left, you hold on to Jesus' own oath that **"I am with you always, to the very end of the age"** (Matthew 28:20).

He is standing up for you, just as he did when he hung on a cross for you. He is loving you, just as he did when he bled and died for you. He is eager to experience with you the same glory Stephen enjoyed *while stones were pelting him.*

Did you catch that?

As rock after rock was chipping away at his life, there's no mention of Stephen feeling any of the pain. The Bible only mentions the glorious sight of Jesus and Stephen's conversation with him.

I've been by the bed of dying Christians enough times to know by the testimony of my own eyes that Jesus stands up for his disciples in a very special way when their earthly lives are ending. In many cases, Christian men, women, and children who ought to be in tremendous pain in their last moments enjoy an obvious feeling of perfect peace. I can't tell you in every case what they were seeing at the moment (though I could come pretty close in some cases), but it was clear to me they were seeing the fulfillment of God's promise in Revelation 2:10: **"Be faithful, even to the point of death, and I will give you life as your victor's crown."** They continued to stand in faith all the way to death, and God gave them life.

It seems that Shadrach, Meshach, and Abednego enjoyed the certainty of that life and its glory even before they died. Even as they were (mistakenly) assured their deaths were near. At the very least, thoughts of death didn't trouble them.

They don't need to trouble us either, not when we believe in a God for whom overcoming death, raising people from the dead, comforting his disciples as they were dying, and even rising again from his own death had all become a pretty common mode of operating for him by the time we get to the morning of Jesus' resurrection.

So keep standing up for Jesus. In a world of great unbelief, fear, worry, and doubt, in some way you'll stand out. The world will be better because you do, because more people will have a chance of seeing Jesus through you.

Review Daniel 3:7-12.

Real Life

Johnny was a doctor who lived in a country where Christians are openly persecuted. It was risky for Johnny to speak openly about his Christian faith. One day he and some coworkers were having lunch in the public square when the conversation turned toward a divisive political topic, and soon everyone was talking very loudly, shouting to get their points across. The tone and volume of the conversation was distracting to many around them, and others were paying attention. At one point, one of Johnny's coworkers shouted very loudly, "Hey, Johnny's a Christian. I'd like to hear him say what Christians think about this!"

1. What good reasons might Johnny have had for sharing his thoughts?

2. Can you think of any good reasons why it might have been wise not to share his thoughts?

Questions

1. Do you think it's significant that there were three men who stood together? Do you think the situation would have gone differently if Shadrach, Meshach, or Abednego were at the dedication alone?

2. Which people in your life would stand with you when you stand up for God? Find a time and a way to thank them for their faith.

Hint: If you're having troubling thinking of someone, remember you don't have to know the person personally to know that they would stand with you if they were there. Jesus would stand with you. So would all his disciples. So would everyone in heaven. So would many others on earth—including me.

DAY 9: WHAT GOD CAN SAVE?

Open Your Bible
Read Daniel 3:13-18.

I spent a day at the beach with some friends once. It was part of a larger trip in winter to a location that was much sunnier and warmer than the much colder one from which we had traveled. The day was everything I was hoping it would be—sunny and warm with water nearby. At the end of the day though, I learned something about sunscreen: It's a good idea to use a lot of it when you're in the sun for an extended period of time, as I was that day.

That's one of the many life lessons I've learned the hard way. I ended up with the worst sunburn I have ever experienced. We had a 2.5-hour drive back to our place that night (we were hosted by the parents of one of my friends). I did my best not to move during the entire drive back to the house since any movement, no matter how slight, would cause my charred skin to scream at the rest of my body for making it do anything.

When we arrived at the house, our hosts had a friend there who, upon seeing my sunburned condition, offered me some advice on how to get rid of the pain as quickly as possible. "Run a washcloth under scalding hot water," he said. "When it's completely soaked, rinse it out and quickly press the hot washcloth directly against your sunburned skin. The heat of the washcloth will absorb the heat in your skin, taking away the pain," he promised.

He seemed to believe what he was saying, but I was skeptical. I didn't tell him that. I thanked him for his kind suggestion and got ready for bed, but I didn't sleep. The pain from my sunburned skin only increased as the night went on. Having tried everything I knew in order to minimize the pain, I tried one more thing. I went into the bathroom and found a washcloth. I ran it under scalding hot water until it was soaked. I rinsed it out and quickly pressed the hot cloth against my sunburned skin. Then I did it again on a different part of my skin. And again. And again. And again, until I realized it wasn't working. It only made the pain worse.

There was no fix for the pain. There was no way to avoid it. I couldn't go back to the beginning of the day and apply more sunscreen. I just had to endure it. So I did.

Shadrach, Meshach, and Abednego did have a way to avoid the potential burning pain of King Nebuchadnezzar's furnace—even after they had made the seeming "mistake" (in the eyes of some) of not worshiping the image the king had placed in front of them. The king himself even gave them a solution to the problem to keep them from suffering the fiery fate that had already been promised to them: **"When you hear** [the music]**, if you are ready to fall down and worship the image I made, very good. But if you do not**

worship it, you will be thrown immediately into a blazing furnace. Then what god will be able to rescue you from my hand?" (verse 15).

"What god?" Nebuchadnezzar asked.

"The God we serve is able to deliver us from it," they responded (verse 17).

Notice something: They didn't say, "We *know* he is going to deliver us from it." They didn't know he would. They only believed he *could*.

"But even if he does not, we want you to know, Your Majesty," they went on, **"that we will not serve your gods or worship the image of gold you have set up"** (verse 18).

Pay close attention to that answer because it teaches us so much of what faith really is. So many people go through life treating God like a vending machine. To get what you want from a vending machine, you put in the correct amount of change, press the right buttons, and you receive exactly the thing you were expecting.

What does that look like with God? "If I say the right prayer . . . if I do the right thing . . . if I'm obedient enough . . . faithful enough . . . if my faith comes across to God in just the right way . . . if I don't mess up too much, then God will do what I expect of him. And if he doesn't, well . . ."

You wouldn't be the first person to give up on God because he didn't do what you were expecting, because he didn't permit you to control his actions, because he didn't let you dictate the terms of the relationship, because he didn't allow you to be God.

"Our God is in heaven; he does whatever pleases him," Psalm 115:3 says. "Whatever" means "whatever." It means we don't get to dictate what God does. Ever. It means we trust him entirely. Completely. Totally. We don't get to dictate whatever he does or does not do. We don't get to dictate what he allows in our lives or how he does or does not answer our prayers. And he has certainly earned that right.

Jesus had a way out of his pain too. As bad as my sunburn hurt, how much worse would it feel to have nails pounded through your skin after the sensitive nerves that normally protected it were exposed to the open air after a whip ripped through it a couple dozen times in rapid succession? Jesus could have just stayed in heaven. After he came, he could have chosen to leave before the suffering.

"He does whatever pleases him." And when we consider his wounds, his broken skin, his pain-filled cries on the cross to which he was nailed, what we see is that what pleased him most was to love you and me, to stay by our sides no matter what it cost him. He did this to save us and to assure us that all the times we have wanted to be God instead of worshiping him and trusting him—are forgiven.

Then Jesus rose from his grave on Sunday morning to show us that he really is able to lead us to a better place no matter what this troubled world might ever take away. In fact, he's not just able. He'll come through for you and me. We can trust God. **"I am the resurrection and the life,"** Jesus said. **"The one who believes in me will live, even though they die"** (John 11:25).

Shadrach, Meshach, and Abednego believed. That's why they weren't afraid of the fire. They believed that whatever God chose to do for them in the next few moments, he for sure would not fail to love them forever.

"What god will be able to rescue you?" Nebuchadnezzar asked. Yours.

Review Daniel 3:13-18.

Real Life

Emily was in the hospital facing a life-threatening illness. She prayed to God for healing. A nurse overheard her prayer and said to her, "God is going to do one of two things in answer to your prayer. He's either going to make you better, or he's going to make you perfect. One of those happens on earth. The other only happens in eternity with Jesus."

1. Was that a good thing for the nurse to say to Emily? Why or why not?

2. Who in your life has helped you see that God is trustworthy? How did they do that? Was it something they said, or was it the way they lived?

Questions

1. King Nebuchadnezzar believed he was God, or at least more powerful than the God of Shadrach, Meshach, and

Abednego. Where in the world today do you see the same type of attitude?

2. In what types of situations do you see Christians trying to control God rather than trust him? How might you help such people trust God better?

3. **"God is in heaven; he does whatever pleases him"** (Psalm 115:3). Is this comforting to you, or does it make you fearful? Explain your answer.

GOD UNDERSTANDS

DAY 10: YOU'RE NEVER ALONE

Open Your Bible
Read Daniel 3:19-27.

A hospital was recently looking for volunteers to cuddle with newborn babies. Not all the babies, though. Just the babies who were born already addicted to drugs. Some babies are born this way because they spent the previous nine months attached to the body of a woman who was addicted to drugs. According to one study I saw, the number of babies born already addicted to drugs has increased by 383% in the last 20 years.[1]

Hospitals have developed programs to help these babies recover, but they have found that there is one medication that helps them recover most quickly. Drug-addicted babies who are cuddled for a couple of hours every day go home sooner and beat the addiction much more consistently. These babies need help because they're vulnerable. They need someone to be with them. When someone is, it makes a big difference.

Shadrach, Meshach, and Abednego needed help too. Their bodies weren't overcome by a drug addiction. Their bodies, vulnerable to pain in all the same ways yours and mine are, were about to be tossed into the intense flames of a blazing furnace. But it was actually worse than that!

King Nebuchadnezzar became so angry at these three men for defying him that he ordered the furnace to be heated seven times hotter than usual! It was so hot that the soldiers who tossed them into the furnace were killed by the intensity of the heat! If that's what happened to the men who only got close to the fire, what would you expect would happen to the three men who were actually thrown into it?!

King Nebuchadnezzar certainly didn't expect to see what actually happened. **"Weren't there three men that we tied up and threw into the fire?"** he asked his advisors.

"Certainly, Your Majesty," they replied.

"Look!" he said. **"I see four men walking around in the fire, unbound and unharmed"** (verses 24,25).

Unharmed. When King Nebuchadnezzar called them out of the fire, everyone saw **"that the fire had not harmed their bodies, nor was a hair of their heads singed; their robes were not scorched, and there was no smell of fire on them"** (verse 27). It was as if they were never in the fire to begin with, but they were. It just didn't harm them at all.

What about that fourth man, the one who never came out of the fire? **"The fourth looks like a son of the gods,"** Nebuchadnezzar said (verse 25). He was on to something. For in that fourth man we see God doing for Shadrach, Meshach, and Abednego what Jesus has promised to do for each of us. **"I am with you always, to the very end"** (Matthew 28:20). "Always" means "always."

GOD UNDERSTANDS

When you're by the hospital bed of someone you love. When you've lost your job. When the relationship breaks beyond repair. When the addiction overcomes you again. When you're too weak to keep going. When no one checks to see how you're doing. When you feel alone. When you stand up for your faith and life gets intense as a result. God is there.

Many of us have heard this account of the three men in the fiery furnace so many times that we know exactly how it turns out. But remember that these three men didn't. They fell into the fire fully expecting to be burned and to die. They didn't know they were going to see Jesus that day. They didn't know he was going to protect them in that special way, but they did know he would be with them. You too can be certain that he will always be with you.

How? Remember another day Jesus did not run away from the fire in front of him. It was the day he hung on a cross and died for sins that weren't his as he fell into the fire of a hellish separation from heaven so that we, who give God plenty of reasons to push us away, could approach God's throne of grace completely forgiven and confident that our God's only desire is to love and protect his children.

The particular ways he chooses to do that during your life on earth are sometimes just as evident to your eyes as God's protection of Shadrach, Meshach, and Abednego was to Nebuchadnezzar's eyes. But sometimes the specific ways God protects, loves, and cares for you on earth are mysterious, and you must live by faith—just as these three men did as they fell into the fire in front of them.

The way God will care for you once your days on earth are done is not a mystery, though. **"[God] will wipe every tear from their eyes. There will be no more death or mourning or crying or pain"** (Revelation 21:4). In other words, it will be as if the fires of earthly pain never touched you. You will, of course, know that they did. But in the end, they didn't keep you from enjoying to the most perfect degree everything Jesus lived and died to give you graciously.

"Be strong and courageous. Do not be afraid; do not be discouraged, for the Lord your God will be with you wherever you go" (Joshua 1:9).

"Wherever" means "wherever." *Wherever* you go.

"Will" means "will." God *will* be with you.

You are never alone.

Review Daniel 3:19–27.

Real Life

Mark unexpectedly lost his job. He had moved far away from his family many years ago to pursue this job, a decision his family didn't fully support, though they wished him well. He had connected with a local church he enjoyed early on, but he disengaged months ago when work demands increased.

1. Before Mark decides what to do, what's something about God that might be helpful for Mark to remember or believe? Think in particular about the characteristics

of God revealed in the Bible (things that help you understand what God is like) or promises God gives you to believe.

2. If you were Mark, what would be the heaviest burden you think you would be carrying in this situation? Joblessness? Family issues? Spiritual weakness? Guilt? Something else?

Questions

1. King Nebuchadnezzar responded with intense anger to the faith of these men. Do you see the same type of reaction to Christians in the world today? If so, where?

2. What do you see as the primary way Shadrach, Meshach, and Abednego shared their faith with the king? Through their words, through their actions, or something else?

3. Finish this sentence in a way that's true: It's obvious Shadrach, Meshach, and Abednego trusted God because . . .

4. Finish this sentence in a way that's true: One way I can show the people in my life that I trust God is . . .

DAY 11: YOUR HEART MATTERS

Open Your Bible
Read Daniel 3:28-30.

Can I ask you something? I want you to think about your answer for a bit before you write anything down or share your answer with anyone. Ready? Here's the question (don't forget to pause and think): How do you know you're really a Christian?

I don't know if that was an easy question for you to answer or if you're still thinking, but I'll come back to that question. Don't forget your answer. For now, I want you to imagine you're hanging out with some friends in a public place. Your group starts talking with another group that's hanging out in the same place. No one in either of your groups has ever met before, but you all get along easily as the conversations start flowing, and you end up making some new friends.

At one point during the night, the conversation turns toward religion. You tell your new friends that you're a Christian, and one of the guys in the other group asks, "So am I going to hell?"

"What do you mean?" you ask.

"Well," he goes on, "I'm married in a homosexual relationship. Don't Christians believe that all homosexuals are going to hell? Do you really think that homosexuality is a sin and a serious one?"

Let's imagine that you do tell him that homosexuality is a sin, as the Bible says it is. It is just as much a sin against God as lying, cheating, arrogance, greed, or physical intimacy between a man and a woman who are not legally married. (By the way, do you know what all those sins have in common? They're all real sins that many real Christians struggle with far more than they were ever hoping they would—but that's a topic for another day). Back to the conversation . . .

Let's imagine that after some back and forth, you are somehow able to convince him that homosexuality is wrong. He believes it now. His plan is to go home, tell his husband that they can't do this anymore because it's not God-pleasing, and have a judge annul the marriage. Wow. You weren't expecting that, but that's what happened.

Let's also imagine that the name Jesus never comes up at any point in your conversation with him. He doesn't believe that Jesus is the Savior of the world who loves him and forgives his sins. If that's what the man believes (or doesn't believe) when he dies, does that person who is now determined to follow God's rule end up in hell or heaven?

He ends up in hell because whoever does not believe in Jesus as the Savior of the world **"will be condemned."** Jesus said that in Mark 16:16. We are saved by the perfect work of Jesus as our Savior, and we are connected personally to the benefits of that work by faith in him. We're not saved by following the rules.

Why am I bringing that up at the end of Daniel chapter 3? Do you remember what just happened? Shadrach, Meshach, and Abednego stood up for their God. They stood firm in their faith—and they were "rewarded" with an all-expenses-paid trip to King Nebuchadnezzar's fiery furnace. But instead of dying, God stepped into the fire right alongside them, protecting them completely from any kind of damage or pain.

King Nebuchadnezzar was so amazed at what had happened that he praised their God and decreed that anyone in his country who worshiped any god but theirs would **"be cut into pieces and their houses turned into piles of rubble"** (verse 29). In other words, he commanded everyone to follow God. Whether or not they really wanted to. Whether or not they loved him. Whether or not they believed in the Savior who was coming.

Nebuchadnezzar's reaction was great!

But how do you know you're a Christian?

If your previous answer had something to do with how well you do something—following God, obeying his rules—even unbelievers on their way to hell can do that, sometimes even better than people who call themselves Christians.

Some years back, I remember reading about a dog that had gone missing in the city of Winkongo, which is in the country of Ghana. This was apparently very surprising to the owner because the dog was very loyal, perfectly obedient, very responsible, and had never run off on its own before. It had been trained to stay on the property. That was the rule, and it knew the rule. One night though, the dog had been missing for several hours. So the owner gathered a search team to go looking for him. They were out most of the night when they finally found him sitting underneath a bridge. When they called to him, he wouldn't move. As they got closer, they discovered why. The dog was snuggled up against a newborn baby with the umbilical cord still attached. The cord was torn and infected, and the baby was severely dehydrated. Even though it had been a cold night, the baby was warm and alive because the dog had snuggled up against it.

If you're the owner of that dog, do you get angry at your dog for not following the rule? Of course not. You're glad it didn't, because *not* following the rule saved the infant.

There was a day in Jesus' ministry when he celebrated the breaking of a godly rule. It was in the Old Testament. King David and his men were on the run for their lives when they came to the temple. There they ate the consecrated bread that was absolutely off limits to anyone but the high priest, who willingly gave it to them.

But Jesus was good with what they had done. Even though they broke the rule, the high priest didn't violate the law. David and his men were hungry. They were famished. Maybe they could have died. So to help them rest and recover, the priest gave them the only bread he could find, and they ate it. God had no problem with it.

God didn't give us his laws so we could prove how good

we are at following the rules or so we could say, "Look, God! We're really good Christians." He gave us his laws knowing how often we would need to say the opposite.

Just think about the last time your sinfulness was exposed like that little baby in the cold, the last time you were caught in a sin, the last time you remembered you can't hide anything from your Father in heaven, the last time you were alone in the dark with a heavy and guilty heart, wondering if God could really love someone like you because you know exactly the kinds of things you've thought and craved leading up to that moment.

At those times, there is one thing more important than asking yourself how you know you're a Christian. It's asking, "How does God know?" and then watching his perfectly obedient Son go to a cross. There he was abandoned, dehydrated, had his skin torn open, and was infected with the sins of the world so that your heart could be warmed with the truth that when God answers the question of whether or not you're a Christian, he doesn't look at what you do or do not do. He only looks at what Jesus did. He always comes to the same conclusion—that you're so thoroughly forgiven of everything that all he sees when he looks at you is perfection, that you don't need to wonder anymore if you're a Christian. In Christ Jesus, you just are. God's not sitting in heaven evaluating you. He's loving you. He truly does want your tired heart to be at rest today.

And you love him for it! He won your heart by that love. Sure, he wants your obedience—for your own sake! He sets up rules to protect you from yourself. That's why he gave Adam and Eve rules in the very beginning. He knew what would serve them well. He knew better than they did. But more than anything, God wants your heart.

So think about how you use God's rules in your relationships. If the primary impression you and I give our children, spouses, friends, neighbors, or parents is that we're constantly evaluating them, that our love for them depends on how well they follow the rules or meet our expectations, we're not relieving the pressure on their tired hearts. We're increasing it because we're teaching them to pay more attention to what they do and less attention to what Jesus did for them. We're teaching them to be afraid of something God intended only to bless his children. That's why he commands us never to give up meeting together in worship, as some are in the habit of doing. That's why he commands us to plant ourselves in his Word as regularly as a tree planted by a stream drinks in the water. That's why he commands us to pray without ceasing, to be compassionate and generous and forgiving.

God believes these are the very best ways for us to be blessed. Or, to say it another way, God knows that every aspect of our lives is always better off in his hands. Following his laws is how we show that we know it too.

Review Daniel 3:28-30.

GOD UNDERSTANDS YOUR CHALLENGES

Real Life

Sophia was in the situation described at the beginning of this chapter. When she was asked, "So am I going to hell?" she responded by saying, "I think that's an important question, and I want to hear your thoughts on it. But can I ask you a different question first?"

"Sure," the man replied.

Sophia asked, "Who do you think Jesus is?"

1. Why do you think Sophia chose to ask that particular question? Why would she think it's good to know who Jesus is before she would ask someone to respect what his Word says?

2. What would you say to someone who complains that Sophia's question is really avoiding the topic of accountability to God (read James 2:18 for help).

Questions

1. What is it about Jesus that you love the most?

2. In your opinion, what godly laws do Christians have the most difficult time following today? Why do you think that is?

3. Shadrach, Meshach, and Abednego were more obedient

GOD UNDERSTANDS

to loving God than to loving their own lives because that's obviously what they wanted to do. Why do you think they wanted to do that? Do you think it was more because they were afraid of being punished by God if they didn't or because there was something good about God they didn't want to give up?

GOD UNDERSTANDS YOUR LIMITS

—

Daniel Chapter 4

DAY 12: YOUR KNOWLEDGE IS LIMITED

Open Your Bible
Read Daniel 4:1-19.

Our family enjoys watching different sports. One year we were watching a basketball championship game, but we weren't all watching in the same location. Our kids were watching on a television in Wisconsin while my wife and I were over four thousand miles away in Hawaii.

We were on a video call during the game so we could still watch it together. During the call, I noticed that the television feed my wife and I were watching in Hawaii was at least ten seconds ahead of what our kids were watching in Wisconsin. So we knew what was going to happen before they did.

One of our sons was the first to pick up on this, but being a good brother, he didn't immediately tell his siblings. Instead, he paid attention to our television through the phone and then "predicted" what was going to happen. "I bet he's going to make this free throw," he said.

"Oh, I don't know," the others would say. "He's missed over half of them so far."

But sure enough, the player hit the free throw.

"I bet they're going to pass it to the guy in the corner, and he's going to hit a three," our son would say.

"No way; they should never pass it to him."

But sure enough, it happened. It didn't matter how confident my son was when he said those things, his siblings didn't believe it until they saw it with their own eyes, because they understood a very basic principle of life: Our knowledge is limited.

There is only so much we know about the present. We don't really know as much about what happened in the past as we think when we're going through it. And the future? That's impossible to predict. For us, anyway. Not for God.

King Nebuchadnezzar's dream reminds us of that. In Daniel chapter 4, Nebuchadnezzar had another dream, one that "terrified" him. Again, as was the case with his dream in Daniel chapter 2, he didn't know its meaning, so he asked all the wise men of Babylon to try to interpret it for him. No one could. Not even Daniel (at first). We're told that Daniel, because he didn't know the meaning of the dream—even after Nebuchadnezzar shared the details of the dream with him—**"was greatly perplexed for a time, and his thoughts terrified him"** (verse 19).

The dream was from God, and in it God shared the purpose of the dream with Nebuchadnezzar. God wanted everyone, especially Nebuchadnezzar, to **"know that the Most High is sovereign over all kingdoms on earth"** (verse 17).

What does that mean? It means that from his much higher perspective on all that was, is, and will be—he knows. God knows everything that has happened, is happening, and will happen. But sometimes that is what's most troubling to Christians.

I recently received a text message from a longtime friend who said, "Why does God allow innocent children to be hurt while the vile people who do it walk free?" She was talking about her own child and the horrible pain someone had inflicted on her many years ago without any consequences for him. Meanwhile the vulnerable little victim lives with the damage of what he did.

A little further back, I received an email from another friend in which she used multiple pages to describe the unspeakably painful things that have been done to her and her loved ones over the course of her life. She asked why God, if he knew what was going on, didn't stop any of those things from happening?

Do you know what's true about both of those friends? They're both Christians. They believe in Jesus. They read the Bible, and they read it to their children. That shouldn't surprise you. It's not uncommon for Christians to want God to be more visible than he is sometimes. You and I want to know he's with us. We want to know he's helping. We want to know he cares. But if finding comfort from God is sometimes hard for Christians when life hurts, how much harder is it for those who hurt and don't even have a sliver of hope that God is real and really cares about them? This is especially hard as they live in a world where every hour, on average, five children die from abuse and thousands more die from cancer and traffic accidents; where every 7 minutes a person becomes disabled to the point that they lose their ability to make a living; where every 11 minutes, someone in the world decides that their life hurts so much that they make a decision to end it?[2]

Not everybody hurts all the time, but hurt is always happening. God knows? Yes. "The Most High is sovereign over all kingdoms." God knows. His knowledge is not limited.

Jesus knew he was going to heal a leper of leprosy before he healed him: A man with leprosy came to him and begged him on his knees: **"'If you are willing, you can make me clean.' Jesus was indignant. He reached out his hand and touched the man. 'I am willing,' he said. 'Be clean!' Immediately the leprosy left him and he was cleansed"** (Mark 1:40-42).

Leprosy is an awful self-destroying skin disease. Because leprosy is so contagious and so deadly, lepers at Jesus' time were required to keep their distance from everyone, and all people were required to keep their distance from them. No hugs. No handshakes. No fist bumps. And not just for a time. It was all the time for the rest of the lepers' lives. As lepers endured immense physical pain, they also had to deal with the daily emotional pain of knowing that no one was willing to be close to them. But Jesus was. It's why he touched the leper. Jesus wanted him to know how eager he was to be there with him in the present.

You may have noticed what Jesus *didn't* do while this was happening. When the leper wondered out loud about God's willingness to help him, Jesus didn't shame him for asking the question. When Jesus said compassionately, "I am willing," he was saying that he understood why the leper (and you and me) asked his question. Jesus was acknowledging that living by faith is hard—for all of us.

Why else would we worry about our lives and our ability to care for our loved ones if we didn't wonder if God really could keep his promise to provide all we would ever need?

Why else would we ever be afraid of the unknown future if we didn't wonder if a God who loves us is really overseeing all of history for our benefit?

Why else would we sometimes most eagerly try to get people to notice or appreciate us if we didn't sometimes wonder if God really does deserve all our greatest praise and attention?

Why else would we ever go a day without praying if we didn't wonder if God is really paying attention?

Jesus knows we wonder about many things. He knows our knowledge is limited. I don't know how you typically react when someone doubts you or wonders if you're worth anything, but instead of pushing us away for our wonderings, Jesus did something different.

He did something similar to what a man named Jonathan did. One day he and his teenage daughter were driving across a bridge while running some errands when they were involved in a serious five-car accident. When Jonathan saw that he and his daughter were OK, he got out of his car to see if anyone else needed help, walked toward the truck that was turned over on its side dangling over the edge of the bridge, and was told by the driver that her daughter's car seat had been thrown from the truck into the water below with her little daughter still in it. Sure enough, when Jonathan looked over the edge, he saw the car seat in the water—30 feet down. But the little girl wasn't in it. She was a few feet away, floating face down.

Jonathan was afraid of heights. But when he looked around and saw no one else coming, he ripped off his shoes, made the 30-foot jump into the water, put the little girl over his shoulder, patted her on the back until she started coughing, and carried her to shore where an ambulance was waiting. She lived. Why? Because someone was willing to jump into the place of her pain and save her from it, no matter the risk, no matter what it cost him. Just like Jesus, and not just on the day he touched the leper's skin.

Fast-forward three years from that day to the day Jesus' skin was whipped and beaten. After that happened, Matthew tells us that "[soldiers] **spit on him, and took the staff and struck him on the head again and again.**" Then **"they offered Jesus wine to drink, mixed with gall; but after tasting it, he refused to drink it"** (Matthew 27:30,34). Why did Jesus refuse to drink it? Because he knew what it was. It was a concoction meant to numb the pain of what he was suffering so it wouldn't hurt so much. But he refused it because he wanted the whole world to see exactly where God is when we are hurting. He is hurting right here in this world with us, not avoiding our pain but voluntarily jumping into the worst of it. He was not willing to turn away even when the nails were pounded in, even knowing that his Father really would remain in the stands in heaven and want nothing to do with him if he were to go through with forgiving us for all the times we have doubted his determination to save us from a world of sin. But he did.

We don't know everything. We're not God. But we know *that*. We know what Jesus did. We know we have a future now, a future in which we will be as free from all our pain and hurt and sin as that man was from his leprosy the moment Jesus healed him.

It was all because Jesus did something, which is exactly what our hurting world needs to see very regularly. And if it can't see Jesus easily, then it needs to see his compassionate heart through you and me coming close to people in their pain, acknowledging that we also know how hard it is to live by faith and then showing them the God we have faith in. He is the God we know from his own Word—the One who chose to hurt right alongside them, who is also very much looking forward to the day when we will all know from experience that the Most High—who loves each of us—really is sovereign over all things.

Review Daniel 4:1-19.

Real Life

Liam, a successful businessman, prided himself on knowing the market inside and out. But when an economic downturn hit, he was blindsided. All his expertise couldn't prepare him for the sudden and catastrophic loss. Liam felt desperate and broken.

1. List all the options, both bad and good, you think someone in Liam's position might consider at that moment.

2. If you were to speak with Liam, of which of the following would you remind him first:
   - God's power to do anything
   - God's unfailing love for the whole world
   - God's knowledge of everything in the past, present, and future

Questions

1. Can you think of a situation when you wondered why God did or didn't act in a way for which you were hoping? How did you feel toward God at that time?

2. Agree or disagree: It's easy to live by faith. Explain.

3. Think of someone specific who needs to see Jesus' compassion right now. Think of a specific time and way you will show it to them.

GOD UNDERSTANDS

DAY 13: YOUR ABILITY IS LIMITED

Open Your Bible
Read Daniel 4:19–27.

Matt oversees a website and podcast dedicated to testing and evaluating automobiles. He loves cars. In 2022 he ordered a 2022 Porsche Boxster Spyder in frozen berry metallic, which costs about $123,000. But delivery was severely delayed. After many weeks, he received a phone call with an update on his vehicle, and it wasn't a good one. He posted the update on his social media account, saying, "I just got a call from my dealer. My car is now adrift, possibly on fire, in the middle of the ocean." And he wasn't kidding.

A massive cargo ship holding thousands of cars, including over 1,000 Porches, almost 200 Bentleys, and a couple thousand other not-inexpensive vehicles started on fire. The entire crew was able to get off the boat safely. But the ship and all the vehicles on it were left to burn and drift for about a week in the middle of the ocean. Eventually, Matt got his car—not the one on that boat—but in Matt's mind, that wasn't the way the car-buying experience was supposed to go. And he couldn't stop it from happening.

Matt's not the only one who's ever come to that realization. Except quite often when we come to that same conclusion—that something didn't go the way it was supposed to go and we weren't able to do anything about it—we're thinking about something that's worth more to us than a new car that costs over $100,000. We're thinking about someone's life, either our own or the life of someone we love, that got harder than anyone wanted. We're thinking about a significant relationship that used to be stronger. We're thinking about our world and all the people who get hurt in it for no good reason. We're thinking about someone's health, something that happened to someone who's still so young or someone whose death either will or did make us feel like we're the ones drifting out in the middle of the ocean.

All these different experiences remind us of one sobering truth about ourselves: Our ability is limited.

That was the sobering message God was sending to King Nebuchadnezzar in his dream. In the dream was a large and beautiful tree. **"Its height was enormous . . . visible to the ends of the earth"** (verses 10,11). And it did much good. **"On it was food for all. Under it the wild animals found shelter"** (verse 12). But then a messenger from heaven commanded that the tree be cut down, and it was, leaving only the stump and its roots, which were useless to the animals for which it had been providing shelter and food.

Then the tree was addressed as a **"him,"** and the messenger from heaven commanded that he be **"drenched with** the dew of heaven . . . live with the animals and among the plants of the earth" and "let his mind be changed from that of a man and let him be given the mind of an animal, till seven times pass by for him"** (verses 15,16).

If I didn't know the dream was from God, I'd suggest that whatever he had for dinner the previous night be removed from the royal menu. But the dream was from God, and God eventually made the meaning of the dream known to Daniel.

The tree represented Nebuchadnezzar. **"You have become great and strong,"** Daniel said. **"Your greatness has grown until it reaches the sky, and your dominion extends to distant parts of the earth"** (verse 22). Nebuchadnezzar was as successful as any king in the world could ever be. Babylon was at the height of its power.

Nebuchadnezzar possibly felt like someone who had just been promoted to CEO of a Fortune 500 company. Or a social media influencer who just gained their millionth follower. Or a pastor whose church has been growing rapidly. Or a parent who just oversaw the biggest ever profit at the PTO fundraiser. Or a kid who was picked first by his peers for the game at recess.

None of those are bad things, just like it wasn't bad at all for Nebuchadnezzar to be a successful king of a world power nation. Countless lives were helped because of what he did while he was in that position. But there was one thing even Nebuchadnezzar couldn't control. If God wanted to take it all away, not even Nebuchadnezzar could stop that from happening. He didn't have the ability. And if he didn't have the ability to stop God from taking every good thing in his life away, then he really didn't have as much to do with gaining all those things as he likely imagined. It happened because God allowed it.

"The Most High is sovereign over all kingdoms" (verse 25). Whether that kingdom was Babylon, the PTO planning committee, the school playground, the board room, the church sanctuary, or whatever ground on which you happen to be standing currently.

Nebuchadnezzar didn't think he needed God to live. But he did, and we do. Entirely.

"The God who made the world and everything in it is the Lord of heaven and earth.... He himself gives everyone life and breath and everything else" (Acts 17:24,25). You couldn't breathe without God's permission.

"For you created my inmost being; you knit me together in my mother's womb" (Psalm 139:13). Your body wouldn't function without God's ability to piece you together in a way that makes that happen.

"He causes his sun to rise" (Matthew 5:45). The food we eat, the daily nourishment without which we would quickly die, would never find its way to your belly if God didn't have an ability you and I do not—that of creating an entire universe and making it work. Every day. Day after day. Whether or not we ask it to.

But he did create that universe. And he did piece you together. And he continues to have the sun rise so the plants and foods our bodies need to live continue to grow. Every day. Day after day. Whether or not you ask for it. Whether or not you remember to thank God for it.

Nebuchadnezzar didn't do that. So to remind him of this important perspective, God was going to take away all that Nebuchadnezzar believed his own ability had given him, leaving the king to feel just like any other vulnerable, weak, starving animal every day on the brink of no longer existing. Or like a three-year-old boy falling out of a third-story window.

That's what happened in Los Angeles one day. A three-year-old boy climbed out on the ledge of his family's third-story apartment building. Someone had apparently left a window open, didn't notice when the little boy climbed out of it, and didn't get there in time to stop him from crawling over the edge and falling toward the ground beneath him.

That was the same day Konrad and Jennifer were moving out of that same apartment building. They happened to be carrying their mattress outside to the moving truck when they noticed people were looking up at their building and pointing. They turned their heads just in time to see the three-year-old falling, and they dropped the mattress. Konrad caught the boy in his arms, tumbled on to the mattress, and saved the boy. The kid didn't have a scratch on him.

I don't know that you can be more vulnerable than that little boy who was falling through the air. Yet he was completely OK because someone who had the ability to save him did.

Don't forget that Jesus has done the same thing for you,

and he knew how far he would have to fall in order for that to happen. Our Creator was killed by the creation he loves—not because he was too weak or didn't have the ability to keep his life going. It was because he wanted to show people like you and me just how much of his ability he is always willing to use and how much of himself he is always willing to give to wash us clean of any record of moral inability. He can lead you home through this unpredictable existence to the only place where peace and rest and joy and success with Jesus are all you will ever know.

He gives us everything.

Life.

Breath.

Sun.

Himself.

All that he is.

All his ability.

All his love.

And who better to help the world find it than us since we've seen just how much we all need it. **"Have the same mindset as that of Christ Jesus"** (Philippians 2:5), because it's through us that people find him. We can never be him. We don't have the ability. But more and more, we can come to him in worship and in his Word, find our own healing from him, and then confidently get back up on our feet each day as if God himself is determined to use all that he is to walk with us every step of the way. Because he is.

Review Daniel 4:19-27.

Real Life

Caroline, a mother of three, felt she had to do everything perfectly. She worked hard to juggle work, family, and church commitments while also staying faithful to an intense exercise schedule. But she never felt satisfied with herself. Hiding that personal disappointment from others took a lot of effort. She didn't want to admit she wasn't doing well. One day, it was all too much to carry.

1. How might it comfort her to be reminded that we don't have God's ability to do anything as well as God could? Or that even the apostle Paul once admitted life was too much for him to handle? **"We were under great pressure, far beyond our ability to endure, so that we despaired of life itself"** (2 Corinthians 1:8).

2. How might it comfort her to know that God allowed the apostle Paul to be overwhelmed in life to teach Paul not to **"rely on ourselves but on God, who raises the dead"** (2 Corinthians 1:9)?

3. Which of the following biblical truths would you share with Caroline first?

    - God chose to give her life, to knit her together in her mother's womb.

- Jesus chose to give his own life for her on a cross, forgiving her of every mistake and guaranteeing her a place in eternity with God.

Questions

1. What is the biggest source of stress in your life right now? As you feel comfortable, share your answer with someone.

2. First Peter 5:7 says, **"Cast all your anxiety on [God] because he cares for you."** God wants to use his ability to help you. Offer a prayer to God asking him to do just that with the things that stress you right now.

3. Think of someone you know who is stressed. Offer another prayer to God asking him to care for them. Then reach out to that friend and let them know you're thinking of them.

GOD UNDERSTANDS

DAY 14: *MY* HEART IS LIMITED

Open Your Bible
Read Daniel 4:28–33.

It's only happened once that a guy took off his shirt during a pastoral counseling session with me. His name wasn't Kent, but that's what I'll call him. He was in one of my youth Bible classes nine years earlier, which is about the last time I saw him at church. But one Sunday he showed up, and something was obviously wrong when I approached him after worship to say hi. His eyes were swollen and red from crying, and he wouldn't look me in the eye.

We went into a meeting room, and I asked him what was going on. "I'm in real trouble, man," he said. But he wouldn't tell me why. So I tried applying some of what he would have heard in church that morning, but he still wouldn't share any particulars of what type of trouble he was in or what he was really feeling. He stopped crying eventually and then said he was going to go. Before he walked out the door, I gave him a hug—a good, strong guy hug.

And then he started yelling at me.

"Why are you hugging me like that!?" he shouted. "Nobody hugs me like that!" Then the tears started flowing again. He began to weep, very loudly. "Why are you hugging me like that?" he shouted.

"Because I care about you," I answered.

"Nobody cares about me . . . but you do," he eventually acknowledged. "I know you do."

Then he pulled away from me, and he saw the pin I was wearing. I had received a pin from my daughter the previous Christmas. It read, "The Armor of God." And then his eyes lit up. "Pastor," he said, "I gotta show you something." He walked back into the corner of the room so that no one could see him through the meeting room window. He took off his shirt, and covering the entire right side of his waist was a tattoo of Ephesians chapter 6—the "armor of God" section in the Bible:

> **Put on the full armor of God, so that you can take your stand against the devil's schemes. For our struggle is not against flesh and blood, but against the rulers, against the authorities, against the powers of this dark world and against the spiritual forces of evil in the heavenly realms. Therefore put on the full armor of God, so that when the day of evil comes, you may be able to stand your ground, and after you have done everything, to stand. Stand firm then, with the belt of truth buckled around your waist, with the breastplate of righteousness in place, and with your feet fitted with the readiness that comes from the gospel of**

peace. In addition to all this, take up the shield of faith, with which you can extinguish all the flaming arrows of the evil one. Take the helmet of salvation and the sword of the Spirit, which is the word of God. (verses 11-17)

He had tattooed that entire section on his waist. Yes, every word of it. As he was putting his shirt back on, I asked him, "Is that you?"

"Is what me?" he asked.

"Your tattoo," I said. "Does that describe you? Are you someone who puts on the full armor of God regularly?"

He started crying again, but this time there was a deeper pain behind it. And this time he didn't hide anything. Among other things, he went on to tell me how he made money. He was in the business of recruiting young girls to violate and destroy their innocent bodies with adult strangers so he could make a little bit of money off them. He organized prostitution.

After he told me that, I pointed to my pin and to the location of his tattoo, and I asked him again, "Is that you?"

He paused, looked down, and said, "I want it to be."

That's a better answer than it seems King Nebuchadnezzar would have given. In Daniel chapter 4, God had given the king another dream. It was about a large tree that got cut down. Once again, God gave Daniel the meaning of the dream, and Daniel was able to tell Nebuchadnezzar what the dream meant. Nebuchadnezzar was the tree—impressively awesome in the eyes of the world . . . and in his own eyes. And that was the problem. Nebuchadnezzar's heart was so full of love for himself that there was no room for God. God sent him the dream, which included the promised consequence of Nebuchadnezzar losing his mind entirely unless he repented, to save Nebuchadnezzar from himself.

Maybe the king initially took the dream seriously. After all, consider all he had witnessed about Daniel's God by this time—the outcome of a veggie diet, the dream about the statue and the rock, the whole fiery furnace incident—none of which would have been forgotten easily by anyone, no matter how full of themselves they were.

So maybe the king initially nibbled on a piece of humble pie. But then a month went by, and nothing happened. He was still king. He was still powerful. His mind was still sharp. Maybe it was just a dream. Then six months went by, and still nothing changed. Then nine months. Then a year.

The book of Ephesians hadn't yet been written at that time, so it's doubtful anyone asked him the question I asked Kent: "Does that describe you?" But if Daniel would have asked any form of it—

Do you think you need God's armor?
Do you think you need God's protection?
Do you think you need God's help?
Do you even want it?

—we know how Nebuchadnezzar would have answered them.

I
My
My
I

One year after Daniel interpreted the dream for Nebuchadnezzar, a year during which absolutely nothing promised in that dream had yet happened, **"as the king was walking on the roof of the royal palace of Babylon, he said, 'Is not this the great Babylon I have built as the royal residence, by my mighty power and for the glory of my majesty?'"** (verses 29,30).

"*I* have built."
"*My* mighty power."
"For the glory of *my* majesty."

A heart that's full of itself leaves no room for God. So God did as he promised:

Immediately what had been said about Nebuchadnezzar was fulfilled. He was driven away from people and ate grass like the ox. His body was drenched with the dew of heaven until his hair grew like the feathers of an eagle and his nails like the claws of a bird. (verse 33)

Don't think God's patience with Nebuchadnezzar meant

he was tolerant of his prideful sin. **"Do not be deceived: God cannot be mocked"** (Galatians 6:7). If there's one attitude God has promised never to reward, it's when we break his First Commandment (you shall have no other gods), when we make ourselves the center of our universe instead of the One who sends dreams and interprets them and can make a highly powerful king into the ugliest and most embarrassing member of the animal kingdom whenever he chooses to do such a thing.

"Humble yourselves, therefore, under God's mighty hand" (1 Peter 5:6) isn't just good advice for Babylonian kings or organizers of prostitution rings. Do you ever look in the mirror and feel the same thing Kent did—shame in what kind of person is looking back in your direction?

Have you ever been hesitant to put on the buckle of truth because you know it would reveal the truth—that you put down God's armor a bit too easily when it comes to a particular temptation?

Maybe you don't feel fearless like Daniel, Shadrach, Meshach, and Abednego did, like someone who knows they're wearing strong armor and are fully protected. Maybe instead you feel fearful—that the next negative comment is going to make you snap again or that you lost your faith long ago and wonder if you'll ever get it back.

Maybe you don't feel protected from Satan. You feel quite vulnerable to his temptations of self-pity, pride, or discouragement. Do you know how it feels to be vulnerable? You wouldn't be the only one.

GOD UNDERSTANDS

Jesus knows, not because he ever sinned, not because he ever looked in the mirror and hated what his image represented. It's because one day on Calvary he chose to put down every piece of armor he was wearing so that his innocent body could be violated and broken by nails and thorns and sin so you and I could benefit from it. He did it so we could be forgiven of everything. Even pride. He did it so we can see an empty grave that gives us the right to know that in the end our weakness and our sins don't win. We do.

That's what Kent was doing when he answered my question. When I asked Kent if Ephesians chapter 6 described him, he said, "I want it to." And then I said this: "Do you know what kind of person would never say what you just did? An unbeliever. Someone who has turned their back on God would never want anything to do with God. But you do. We don't find our peace in how well we wear the armor. We find it in the One who gave it to us in the first place and allows us to put it on and move forward again even after we've fallen."

Then Kent started crying again, but this time because he knew what it was like to be set free from a heavy burden.

If God really can lift a heavy burden off someone like Kent and give him strength and a new desire to live a life in which God is the center of everything—and if God really did send prideful, self-absorbed Nebuchadnezzar the dream so that Nebuchadnezzar could see his sin and be saved from it because that was the only outcome God wanted—then whatever it is you've done, however the weakness of your prideful heart has shown and will ever show itself, you also have the God-given right to get back on your feet and move forward again.

My heart is vulnerable to pride. Yours is too. But God's heart for you is never in question. What his heart compelled him to accomplish for you through Jesus isn't a dream. It's the very best part of your enduring reality.

Review Daniel 4:28-33.

Real Life

Jake, a skilled surgeon, was the talk of the medical world. He was so skilled at what he did that surgeons from around the world asked permission to watch his procedures. When a simple mistake—one that would normally be made by someone much less experienced and skilled—led to the death of a very prominent and well-known celebrity, it ruined Jake's reputation. He was devasted.

1. Do you think pride had anything to do with Jake's mistake? If so, how did his pride reveal itself?

2. How might Jake be tempted to be prideful moving forward as he tries to rebuild his self-esteem and career?

Questions

1. The Bible says, **"The heart is deceitful above all things and beyond cure"** (Jeremiah 17:9). Where do you see

proof of this in the world today? Consider also where you've seen proof of it in your own life.

2. The Bible says, **"If our hearts condemn us, we know that God is greater than our hearts, and he knows everything"** (1 John 3:20). In what way does the work of Jesus apply to this verse? God already knows everything about our hearts. Everything. Yet if his work through Jesus is greater than what's in our hearts . . . (*finish the thought in a way that's true*).

3. Agree or disagree: Pride is a major problem in our world today. Explain your answer.

4. Agree or disagree: The good news of Jesus as the Savior of the whole world is the best antidote to the heart-sickness of pride. Explain your answer.

GOD UNDERSTANDS YOUR LIMITS

DAY 15: GOD'S LOVE IS UNLIMITED

Open Your Bible
Read Daniel 4:34-37.

One of my favorite Olympic moments happened during the 1992 Summer Olympics in Barcelona, Spain. If you remember those Olympics, you probably remember it too.

Derek Redmond was the British 400-meter record holder when he was only 19 years old. He qualified for the 1988 Olympics in Seoul, Korea, and made it into the finals easily. Ten minutes before the most important race of his life, however, Derek's Achilles tendon gave out, and he had to pull out of the race. But he didn't give up on his Olympic dreams. Over the next year, he had five different surgeries to repair his Achilles, began training again, and easily qualified for the 1992 Olympics in Barcelona. In the semifinal race, Derek took the lead very quickly. Halfway through the race, he was a shoo-in to make the finals, until he heard a loud POP! It was his Achilles. He couldn't run. The other runners passed him quickly as Derek collapsed to the track and then tried to hobble his way to the finish line.

Here's the memorable moment: His father was sitting in

the stands. When he saw his son slow down, he knew exactly what had happened and exactly how crushed his son was feeling. He raced down from the stands, leapt over the railing, ignored the repeated commands from the security guards to stop what he was doing, outran them, put his arm around his son, put the weight of his son's hurting body on his shoulders, and walked with him until they crossed the finish line together.

It was a memorable moment when a father didn't let anything get in the way of giving his hurting child the help, attention, support, and love he needed.

I wouldn't blame you if you paused right now and searched for "Derek Redmond 1992 Olympics video" on your computer or personal device. If you're a crier or a parent or a child or an Olympian or a human, you may want some tissues nearby when you watch the video.

Derek lost that race. Badly. Entirely. The time between him crossing the finish line and the runner immediately ahead of him was exactly we-turned-off-the-stopwatch-because-it-was-taking-so-long seconds. Yet no one thinks of Derek's race as a loss. It's a win of the most beautiful kind. No one thinks of Derek as a loser. Just the mention of his name brings a smile to the faces of those who recognize it.

I don't know how you normally think of King Nebuchadnezzar. When we last saw him, he had just been turned into one of the strangest-ever members of the animal kingdom. That was his own fault. God gave Nebuchadnezzar a chance to acknowledge that he was running his race of life in entirely the wrong way. He was full of himself. He was full of pride. He was losing. He had lost.

But that's not the picture of Nebuchadnezzar we are left with in the last few verses of Daniel chapter 4. Nebuchadnezzar praises the Most High. He honors and glorifies **"him who lives forever"** (verse 34). His humanity, sanity, and power are all restored by God as Nebuchadnezzar says, **"Now I, Nebuchadnezzar, praise and exalt and glorify the King of heaven, because everything he does is right and all his ways are just. And those who walk in pride he is able to humble"** (verse 37).

Nebuchadnezzar had learned his lesson. His pride was gone. Nebuchadnezzar was not losing any longer when it came to God. He was winning. He won. This is the end of what we hear about Nebuchadnezzar in the book of Daniel, but I wouldn't be surprised if you'll have the opportunity to ask him about all this when you get to eternity with Jesus.

He won. How did that happen? Easy. Pain and loss. God hurt him.

One day a number of years ago when our kids were young, our oldest daughter came running out to the backyard where my wife and I were. She told us that our youngest daughter had just fallen down the basement stairs.

We had 14 stairs that went down to our basement's concrete floor. Our youngest, who was four at the time, had been hanging a picture on the refrigerator in the kitchen. Once the picture was secured, she slowly backed away from the fridge to observe her work, apparently not knowing that the basement door was wide open. Fourteen stairs. One concrete floor. Not one single bruise or scratch anywhere on her body. One very important lesson learned. Our youngest daughter didn't go anywhere near those stairs for many years unless she had to and unless someone was holding her hand.

Falling down the stairs taught her something. It taught her to be a bit more careful about where she's going, which is something we had certainly told her before. But the pain of falling down the stairs taught her the lesson in a way she was more likely to remember.

God did the same thing with Nebuchadnezzar. God inflicted pain on him to teach him a lesson. Why did he have to inflict the pain? It's because there are some lessons we simply will not learn any other way. Just like we cannot bend or change certain metals without letting them sit in a fire, our hearts don't change easily either. They come into this world only thinking about us at every moment. They are sinful from the time we are conceived (Psalm 51:5) and can't be changed to think only about God without going through pain.

If you doubt that, just try to think of one person in the Bible who took even a moment to praise God when their life was nothing but smooth sailing. You won't find many. You may not find any.

On the other hand, there are plenty of people in the Bible who praised God after 38 years of crippling pain, after decades of slavery under the Egyptians, after a man was blind since his life's beginning, after they nearly drowned, after a widow lost her husband and her son, after Jairus believed he would never see his daughter alive again, after lepers were expelled from their wives and children, and after Mary was controlled by seven powerful demons.

All these people, against their will, lost control and fell down the stairs in some way before they learned the same lesson God was teaching the world when *he* was the one in crippling pain, when *God* was the one who had lost everything, when God was the one begging there to be another way, when the God who can heal cripples and drive out demons and has proven again and again that he can do *anything* decided once to use all his strength and all his power to do *nothing*. He didn't come down from the cross; he didn't stop hurting, because his only desire has been to send you one very important message: He really does love you more than anything, even his own skin.

Jesus on a cross is a memorable moment when a Father didn't let anything get in the way of giving you the help, attention, forgiveness, mercy, and love you needed.

There was a meaning to Jesus' pain. By it, God meant to forgive you and give you a home in which you will never have to hurt again, as well as a promise that until you get there, God really is in control. There is meaning to your pain, whether it is brought into your life through no fault of your own or it's a consequence of your own prideful faults.

God always has one purpose when he walks with you through pain. He longs to bring you closer to him, to help you rely on him more firmly. He leads you through fires of various intensities and types to strip you of all the impurities that separate you from seeing him. He allows you to hunger and thirst so you can taste even more fully the sweet refreshment of hearing him say: **"Do not fear, for I have redeemed you; I have summoned you by name; you are mine. When you pass through the waters, I will be with you. . . . When you walk through the fire, you will not be burned"** (Isaiah 43:1,2). That's a win. That's your win. And its reality doesn't rest on your shoulders.

There's one portion of the Derek Redmond race that makes me laugh every time I watch it. After his father put his son's arm over his shoulder and started supporting Derek on the way to the finish line, a man whom I assume was some sort of security personnel ran up to them and seemed to tell Derek's father that he was not supposed to be there on the track. I don't know what Derek's father said in response, but he said it with a lot of passion and a flick of his hand, and the security guy walked away quickly. Nothing was getting in the way of being there for his son.

Look at Jesus. Look at the cross. Consider all he's carrying on his shoulders. Nothing gets in the way of God loving his children. Nothing.

Review Daniel 4:34-37.

Real Life

Laurie faced a number of health challenges that made her job in a factory difficult. She was going through many different types of medical tests to get an accurate diagnosis of everything that was wrong. She had regular therapy sessions she couldn't miss. Her energy at work was low because of how hard she had to work in those sessions. What was most difficult for her, though, was knowing that her condition was her fault—the result of a bad decision. She had been sending a text message on her phone late one night when she was driving. She hadn't seen that her car was swerving into oncoming traffic. She hadn't seen the other car until it was too late. Thankfully, no one in the other car had been hurt.

1. How might you use the account of King Nebuchadnezzar's restoration to encourage Laurie?

2. What truth about Jesus would you share with her first?

Questions

1. Have you ever learned an important lesson "the hard way"? If so, what was it?

2. What about God would you like to remember more easily/regularly?

3. God's wisdom, strength, grace, and forgiveness are boundless. His love for you in Jesus has no limits. How does that help during the times in life when you face your own limitations?

GOD UNDERSTANDS YOUR LEGACY

—

Daniel Chapter 5

DAY 16: FAITHFUL AND FORGOTTEN

Open Your Bible
Read Daniel 5:1-12.

A man who lives in California was arrested in 2023 at O'Hare International Airport in Chicago. Two United Airlines employees in Chicago noticed an unfamiliar man hanging out in a restricted area, so they approached him and asked to see his ID. The ID he showed them said he was an operations manager at the airport, except the operations manager whose name was on that ID had reported that ID missing three months earlier. The reason his ID was missing is because the man who was holding it in front of the United Airlines employees had stolen it three months earlier.

This man had arrived at O'Hare in October 2022 on a flight from Los Angeles. For some reason, that was the day he became very scared of the worldwide COVID virus and decided he didn't feel safe going home to California again. In fact, the only place he felt safe was right where he was, so that's where he stayed—for three months. He stole the ID so he could get around the airport without any troubles and survived on food he politely begged away from other people who were traveling. He did this for three months before anyone had any idea what he was doing. He lived in an airport for three months completely undetected. No one had any clue he was there.

It's kind of like King Nebuchadnezzar's son, who seems to have had no idea that a man named Daniel existed anywhere in Babylon.

Daniel chapter 5 takes place in the year 539 B.C., some 30 years after the events of Daniel chapter 4. Daniel was now in his 80s. King Nebuchadnezzar, the only Babylonian king this book has mentioned so far, was gone. In his place as king was his son Belshazzar. Belshazzar was in need of someone who could interpret confusing things.

Huh. If only there was someone in Babylon who had already shown that ability—multiple times, within the king's own family. King Nebuchadnezzar had two dreams that troubled him, both of which were from God, both of which communicated a very clear message about Nebuchadnezzar's life, and neither of which could be interpreted by anyone. Except Daniel, after God gave him that ability. Daniel faithfully and courageously stepped in, at great risk to his life, interpreting the dreams and maybe even saving Nebuchadnezzar's soul in the process.

Belshazzar had no idea who Daniel was. It seems that Nebuchadnezzar had told his son about Daniel, but Belshazzar didn't care to remember him. Daniel had been forgotten. Yet it doesn't change the fact that something happened to Daniel most of us hope will never happen to us.

Daniel was forgotten. And that hurts. It's like when you realize it's been longer than normal since any of your kids have called. Or your husband forgot it was your birthday. Or you were overlooked for a promotion though you've been working for the company for much longer than the person who got it. Or you check your social media and see your friend group all hanging out and having a great time, but you obviously weren't invited. Or everyone came for the funeral, but now four months later, they've all gone back to their busy lives. No one calls to check in. Not one person has stopped by.

Seeming to disappear from someone's memory, especially if you believe it shouldn't have happened, can hurt so deeply that most people use a lot of energy to avoid it. I would venture to guess that at least a part, and likely a large part, of the reason you work so hard at anything—work, school, keeping up your appearance—is because you're eager to prove something about yourself. That you're worth something. That you're worth remembering.

I bet I know something about that pursuit, even if I don't personally know you. I know the result of it. No matter how hard you work, no matter how much good you do, no matter how faithful you prove to be, at the end of the day, there's always more to prove. Always. In the minds of so many, and sometimes even in your own mind, you're not always worth remembering.

Something else had taken Daniel's place in Belshazzar's memory bank. Based on the scene given to us in Daniel chapter 5, we can say it was some combination of parties, adultery, drunkenness, and idolatry.

Do you remember why Daniel was in Babylon in the first place? Babylon, many years before this party in Daniel chapter 5, had invaded Judah. In addition to taking Daniel and many of his contemporaries with them back to Babylon hoping to indoctrinate them, they also destroyed the beloved temple in Jerusalem and took many of the beloved and sacred worship vessels to Babylon with them. During this particular party, King Belshazzar ordered that the gold and silver goblets his father had taken from the temple be brought out to join their celebration. Everyone drank from them. Then everyone praised the goblets as their gods.

That's when God reminded them of his existence. God made the fingers of a human hand appear in the middle of the room. Everyone saw them, and everyone saw the strange, unintelligible message they wrote on a wall. We'll examine the meaning of the message in a future chapter. But this strange hand had the same impact on Belshazzar that the divine dreams had on his father, Nebuchadnezzar. Belshazzar was terrified and confused. He summoned the wise men of Babylon and promised great honor and riches to the one who could interpret the message correctly.

But there's one thing he didn't do. He didn't think of Daniel. Daniel, the only person in Babylon's history who had ever interpreted messages from God successfully, had been forgotten. Belshazzar had to be reminded that Daniel existed.

I don't think God was surprised by that. One of the

most frequent commands God gave to his people in the Old Testament was the command to remember. What were they to remember? They were supposed to remember God.

"Remember well what the Lord your God did to Pharaoh and to all Egypt" (Deuteronomy 7:18).

"Remember how the Lord your God led you all the way in the wilderness these forty years, to humble and test you in order to know what was in your heart, whether or not you would keep his commands" (Deuteronomy 8:2).

"You may say to yourself, 'My power and the strength of my hands have produced this wealth for me.' But remember the Lord your God, for it is he who gives you the ability to produce wealth" (Deuteronomy 8:17,18).

"Remember that you were slaves in Egypt and the Lord your God redeemed you" (Deuteronomy 15:15).

Remember God. Remember how he helped. Remember how he saved. Remember what you were without him. They didn't. Time and again, the Bible records the nation of Israel forsaking God for the same things that grabbed King Belshazzar's attention: parties, adultery, drunkenness, and idolatry.

They didn't remember, though they had many

opportunities, just as we do. You may never be at a party where human fingers appear out of nowhere and start writing on a wall, but you live in a world full of people whose unloving actions will eventually force you to reveal if you remember Jesus' command to turn the other cheek, to love your enemies, to pray for those who persecute you, to do to others as you would have them do to you, to only speak what is useful for building others up according to their needs, to restore someone who sins gently, to make sure your words are always seasoned with grace, not to think of yourself too highly, not to worry about your life, not to be afraid, not to be ashamed to suffer for the name of the One who said, **"You are my friends if you do what I command"** (John 15:14).

Remembering doesn't happen accidentally. It is a choice to focus on one thing above all else. I recently heard of a pastor who found himself in a situation where he had to make a clear choice between the value of two different things. It was either him or a little animal that got stuck in a tin can. He was taking a walk in the woods when he saw a small animal that was stuck in a tin can. It was a container that at one point held a chocolate hot cocoa mix, and it seemed that when this hungry little animal stumbled upon it, smelled the subtle remnants of sweet yummy chocolate inside it, it went headfirst into the container and got stuck.

When the pastor saw this, he thought two things: "This poor little creature needs my help, and without my help, it will most likely die." Additionally, he thought, "This will make a great sermon illustration about how Jesus was willing to come to earth and set us free from our self-inflicted, sinful stupidity." (Pastors are always looking for good sermon illustrations.)

So whether it was the value of having a sermon illustration or the value of saving an animal from its hunger-induced stupidity, he decided it was worth setting this animal free. He walked toward the animal to do just that until he got closer to the animal and noticed that it was a skunk.

The pastor had originally considered the possibility that the animal might try to fight back if he tried to set it free and that he might end up with a scar or two in the process. But when he saw the white line and considered the consequences of what was likely to happen to him, he decided the skunk wasn't worth as much to him as remembering you was to Jesus when he knew it was far more than an animal's paw that might slice him.

For Jesus, it was a whip. It wasn't one animal he would have to deal with. It was an entire legion of soldiers who bruised his face and whose spit soiled his skin. It wasn't just the threat of being sprayed by a skunk. It was the certainty that he would carry such a wretched stench from carrying the full weight of the world's sins that his own Father in heaven would want nothing to do with him. Jesus promised he would remember to love you always, and he wanted to show you that he meant it. He is the One who forgives you and paid the necessary price and suffered the necessary pain to make that happen. When he says he will always treat you with grace, he can show you the scars that prove it.

You are not forgotten by Jesus. That's what his scars mean. They mean that something was worth more to Jesus than Jesus, and that something was you. It was giving you the ability to look in the mirror each day and know you are looking at someone who is loved and forgiven. It was giving you the ability to walk through this difficult world knowing that whatever pain it inflicts and whatever good it takes away, it won't get the best of you in the end. You have a Friend who walks with you right now, and you can trust that whatever guidance he preaches to you really is the best option, even if you don't understand it in the moment.

It wasn't easy for him to preach that message. He knows it sometimes isn't easy for you, not only because you aren't as strong as him but because a world that forgot about faithful Daniel and crucified our gracious Jesus will also always leave its mark on those who follow the Savior in faithful and faith-filled obedience.

However those scars show up in your life, they will always reveal two important things. They reveal you to be someone who belongs to Jesus, whose scars are a priceless reminder of his love for you. They reveal you as someone who is in the best position of all to help this misguided world see that there's something worth remembering about a God who places his highest value on people like you and me, who gives you his Word that all the scars on your life and your heart are only temporary while everything Jesus already earned for you, you get to keep into eternity.

How can you help a world see and appreciate that? Be

faithful and ready, just as Daniel was, with whatever opportunities come your way, whether or not anyone gives you recognition and love. You already have both of those from God through Jesus.

Review Daniel 5:1-12.

Real Life

Marta was a stay-at-home mom with four young children. Her husband provided for the family well financially, but he was rarely home on account of working such long hours. When he was home, he was tired, wanted to relax, and demanded that the house be clean when he returned home each day so he could do that easily. He didn't know all that Marta did to care for the children when he was gone, and he never asked her about it. Marta felt invisible to her husband.

1. How might you use Daniel's faithfulness in a difficult environment to encourage Marta?

2. How might you use Jesus' faithfulness to her in a difficult environment to encourage Marta?

3. Which option do you think would be best for Marta moving forward:
   - Continue to serve her husband and children as faithfully as she can

- Talk to her husband about how she's feeling and struggling
- Find someone whom her husband holds in high regard, explain the situation to him, and ask if he would be willing to talk to her husband on her behalf

Note: You can find biblical support for each of these options. The best option may be a combination of them all. When deciding which to do first, discuss the benefits and challenges of each one.

Questions

1. What good truth about God do you wish you more easily remembered? (For example, maybe you wish it were easier to remember that he really has forgiven *all* your sins or that he really does promise to work all things for good).

2. Agree or disagree: It's wrong to seek the approval of others.

3. Can you identify a particular category of people in the world today that is easily forgotten? How might you help them see not only that you remember them but that God does?

DAY 17: IN THE HAND OF GOD

Open Your Bible
Read Daniel 5:13-24.

Once when Rhode Island got pummeled by a massive snowstorm, a ten-year-old boy named Christian decided to do something nice for the doctors and nurses who were working at the local hospital that was near his house. He knew they had been putting in long hours since the beginning of the pandemic. But when it snowed after they had already put in a long exhausting day, they would have to walk out to their cars and begin the long, cold, wet process of wiping the snow off them. So Christian recruited his friend Abbey to save them the effort.

Together, the two of them walked over to the hospital parking lots and started clearing the snow off every car. If a worker used their key fob to start their car or unlock it after their shift was done, Christian and Abbey would run over to that car and work quickly to have it cleared off before the worker got into it. Over the course of many hours, the two kids ended up cleaning off about 80 cars in four different employee parking lots. Many of the workers tried to pay them because they were so grateful for what the kids had done. But Christian and Abbey wouldn't have it. They were glad they were in a position to make a difference.

What we do says something about us. What Christian and Abbey did shows that they're kind, thoughtful, and sacrificial. Christian and Abbey moved so much snow with their hands that in the process of removing it, they had to change gloves multiple times. The gloves they were using became so soaking wet from touching all that snow that their fingers started to freeze, but they didn't stop. They kept going. They kept helping, which says something about them. Something good.

What we do says something about us. As far as we know, the fingers of the hand that appeared in King Belshazzar's party weren't frozen. But God used that hand to reveal this truth to that king: What he was doing was saying something about him, and it wasn't good.

"You . . . have not humbled yourself," Daniel told Belshazzar when Daniel was brought in to interpret the handwriting on the wall (verse 22). Belshazzar exalted himself. **"You have set yourself up against the Lord of heaven,"** and **"you did not honor the God who holds in his hand your life and all your ways"** (verse 23).

Belshazzar was a few moments away from seeing for himself how true that last statement was. It would be the last day of his earthly existence because the God who held Belshazzar's life in his hand would not allow it to keep going.

It can be comforting to us as Christians that our God has the power to end the life immediately of any who oppose him. But it can also be a bit terrifying when we try to answer the question: What do your actions say about you?

- *I'm good.* That may be one thing you'd try to say. You may even point to certain things you do in your life to back it up. You read your Bible, you go to church, you're nice to others, and you give offerings. Those are good things. But they sound very similar to the types of things the Pharisee in Luke chapter 18 pointed out about himself as he was praying: **"I fast twice a week and give a tenth of all I get"** (verse 12). He exalted himself, just like Belshazzar did. According to Jesus, that Pharisee was not "justified" before God.

- *I'm better than others.* This is another way you might evaluate what you're doing and what it says about you—by comparing the good things you do to someone else's seemingly worse things. You believe you are more deserving of God's kindness than someone else.

Most Christians won't say this directly since most Christians believe that each person is equally deserving of God's wrath and punishment. But if this attitude is present, as was the case for the Pharisee in Luke chapter 18, it will show up in our relationships. It will usually be accompanied by phrases like, "Can you believe what they just did?" Or, "I can't believe that someone would ever . . ." "I can't believe what those robbers, evildoers, and adulterers do," the Pharisee said. "I can't believe what you did to me." "I can't believe what that politician believes." "I can't believe that someone would walk into a mall and shoot someone."

Of course, it's not wrong to be disgusted by sin or even to condemn it publicly. What's wrong is what the Pharisee did. He used someone else's sin as an opportunity to exalt himself by comparison. To let someone know "I would never . . ." is yet another way someone might try to exalt themselves while being on the outside of God's kingdom looking in.

- *I believe in Jesus.* "I know I'm a Christian because I believe in Jesus as my Savior." That's not a wrong statement to make. It's actually very good if you say that willingly. But I'm going to suggest that the way this phrase is worded puts you on shaky ground—if your basis for knowing you belong to God is by looking at how well you believe in him.

  It's most likely that when you and I say something like that, we're thinking of our faith on one of our better days: when we do a good job of putting our faith into practice, when we're holding tightly to God's promises, when we're remembering every one of his laws, when we're doing a good job resting in his Word—because those are the kinds of things someone who knows they believe in Jesus would do.

But then you have to come up with something to say on the days that you don't do a good job of all those things: when your faith is shaky, when your doubt and fear are high, when you don't remember what God's Word says about how to be patient and kind or you don't care, when someone could rightly ask you, "Does someone who believes in Jesus really act like *that*?" At the very least, putting your confidence in how clearly you believe in Jesus will always leave room for a lot of doubt, which is something the other person in Jesus' story, a tax collector, did not have at all. As he thought of himself, he had zero doubts about his faith. He knew it was poor. He knew it was lacking. It's why he tucked himself away in a corner and didn't feel like celebrating himself in front of anyone. He asked God to have mercy on him, a sinner.

Doing that was an indicator that he felt spiritually how a blind man in Philadelphia once felt physically. His name was Cecil. Cecil was 60 years old, and he was blind. One Tuesday he was waiting for a train on his way to the dentist when he suddenly became faint, started stumbling toward the edge of the platform, and fell down to the train tracks. Just a few seconds later, an express train came speeding around the corner. When the driver of the train saw Cecil there between the tracks, he slammed on the brakes to try and stop the train before it went over him. But he couldn't. The train was already moving too fast.

Do you know what would not have been useful at all to Cecil at that moment? It would not have helped him one bit to think, "I'll be OK because at least there are many times in life that I didn't stumble onto the tracks." It also wouldn't have helped to think, "Well, I fell onto the tracks once, but think of all those clumsy people who have stumbled onto the tracks multiple times. I'm sure glad I'm not like any of them." Neither would it have helped to think, "If I do a good job believing the train won't hit me, then it won't."

The train was coming, just as certainly as King Belshazzar was going to die that evening and just as certainly as you will too one day. That doesn't make you unique in the world. That makes you the same as every king, robber, adulterer, mass shooter, Pharisee, politician, and tax collector, which is why the tax collector didn't feel like celebrating himself in front of anyone. Like Cecil, he was stuck. His life said something about him. He was helpless to help himself, but he was not alone. Just like Cecil wasn't alone as he was lying on those tracks.

His Seeing Eye dog, a black Lab named Orlando, was there with him and tried to stop him from going over the edge when he realized what was happening. When he saw his master fall down, Orlando jumped down after him, lay down next to him between the tracks, and refused to leave his side, even when he saw the train coming. Do you know what Orlando did there? He had mercy on Cecil. To have mercy is to see someone who needs help and to jump in, whether or not they deserve it and whether or not it's going to cost them something. Orlando just kept licking Cecil's face over and over, again and again, as if to tell him it was going to be OK.

And it was. The train *didn't* stop in time, but Cecil and Orlando were lying down flat enough and far enough down between the tracks that the car and a half that passed over them before the train stopped really did pass *over* them. Orlando and Cecil walked away completely unscathed, feeling much the same way the tax collector did when he finished praying.

The tax collector was safe. Why? Because the God to whom he was praying is a God of mercy. He knows how much we will always hurt when we compare ourselves to Jesus, who never used his hands to pat himself on the back or push others down by comparison. Jesus knew how much it would hurt him to jump into our world and place himself in front of the deadly express train of a cross that would only stop speeding when we all stop sinning. And yet he did it.

Unlike Orlando and Cecil, Jesus didn't walk away completely unscathed. Because he didn't, we now know just how long he will stay by the side of anyone who calls themselves a sinner because they know just how much they deserve it.

Jesus will stay to the very end. That gives you the fourth way you can look at a life and evaluate it. Instead of using your hands to pat yourself on the back, instead of pointing to how your uniquely sinful life compares to the uniquely sinful life of another person, instead of pointing to how well you believe in someone, you can point to the Someone God gave you to believe in. He's the One whose nail-pierced hands don't make you wonder if you're forgiven, loved, and guaranteed to live even though you die. You are completely covered now by the perfection of the Christ you are blessed to believe in. By looking at his life, death, and resurrection, there is zero doubt that you simply are. You *know* that by looking at *him*.

What you and I do certainly says something about us. We need help. We need mercy. But what Jesus did with his life says something about us too. We have help. We've received mercy already, and we'll never be without it.

That's the comfort we find in Daniel's explanation of the handwriting on the wall. He reminded Belshazzar that his God, our God, *the* God is the one **"who holds in his hand your life and all your ways"** (verse 23). Your life and all your ways are held in the hand of God.

For all who know Jesus, that's comforting. "I know my sheep," Jesus said in John chapter 10. **"I give them eternal life, and they shall never perish; no one will snatch them out of my hand"** (verses 27,28).

Review Daniel 5:13-24.

Real Life

Anna was a self-described workaholic. She prided herself on pouring all her energy into her highly successful and prominent career. She knew she left her husband and kids behind frequently, regularly not seeing them for days at a time. It had been years since she had seen her parents. She told herself it was worth it. One day she received a phone call that her father had died unexpectedly. Anna was crushed. Nobody supported her like her father did. He's the one who showed her Jesus most faithfully, even when she was too busy to listen.

1. What do you think hurt the most for Anna?

2. Do you think that working hard at the expense of family and faith is a temptation into which many Christians fall? Explain your answer.

3. How would focusing on the life of Jesus help Anna moving forward?

Questions

1. Evaluate the three shaky options/phrases for finding peace with your own life. Which one connects with you most easily? Explain your answer.

   - I'm good.

- I'm better than others.
- I believe in Jesus.

2. Write your own phrase that reliably provides you peace as you think about your life. (Hint: Make Jesus the subject of the sentence.)

3. Belshazzar ignored God's hand, but Jesus extended his hands in love on a cross to redeem you. His hands, pierced for your sins, now hold your life securely. Explain what that means to you.

DAY 18: PAST-PRESENT-FUTURE

Open Your Bible
Read Daniel 5:25–29.

I'd like you to spend some time considering three things:

Identify something in the past that still troubles you.

Identify something in the present that's making life difficult.

Identify something about the future that worries you.

We'll come back to what you've identified in a moment. For now I'd like to tell you something that happened not long ago in California. A woman was home with her family when she heard a noise coming from the backyard. When she walked toward the window and looked into the yard, she saw a mountain lion holding her dog in its mouth by the neck. Thinking quickly, she grabbed the keys to her car and drove it into the backyard right toward the mountain lion, which caused the mountain lion to drop the dog immediately and run away.

The threat was gone. The dog was safe. How did that happen? It wasn't because the woman was so strong but because she brought into the troubling situation something that was bigger and stronger than the threat she and her dog were facing.

In a sense, that is what Daniel did when he shared with King Belshazzar the interpretation of the handwriting on the wall. Daniel was introducing Belshazzar to something that was bigger and stronger than *him*. And not just a part of him. All of him. Past. Present. Future.

The inscription on the wall spelled out the following strange words that the king's wise men could neither read nor explain its meaning to him: "MENE, MENE, TEKEL, PARSIN" (verse 25).

And this was Daniel's explanation of their meaning:

Mene: **God has numbered the days of your reign and brought it to an end.**

Tekel: **You have been weighed on the scales and found wanting.**

Peres*: **Your kingdom is divided and given to the Medes and Persians.** (verses 26-28; **Peres* is the singular form of the word *parsin*.)

God was telling the king that his entire life and entire reign—all that he is, was, and ever could be—was subject to God's judgment, evaluation, and will. That wasn't good news for the king:

Tekel—Your past hasn't lived up to God's standards.

Mene—Your present day is going to be your last day, and you won't be able to do anything to stop it from happening.

Parsin—Everything you've gained and accomplished has no future.

Why was this going to happen? Because if someone would have asked King Belshazzar to identify something about the past that troubled him, something in the present that made life difficult, or something about the future that worried him, there was one answer he seemingly wouldn't have considered. Himself.

Of course, that isn't the only possible answer to those questions. But it is an important one to acknowledge for one simple reason: Belshazzar and you and I are not God. If we were, there would be nothing about our pasts that would trouble us because we wouldn't have made any mistakes and we wouldn't be fearful of any judgment or punishment. As God, we wouldn't be accountable to anyone but ourselves.

If we were God, there would be nothing in the present that would be too difficult for us since we would be *God*, and as such, we would certainly be able to handle anything life threw in our direction.

If we were God, nothing about the future would worry us since as God, we could do anything. We could snap our fingers and change easily whatever needed changing or fix whatever needing fixing.

But we're not God. Our pasts prove it—people we've hurt, the lines we've crossed when no one but God was looking. Jealousies and self-indulgent lusts can easily get the best of us in the present. The times we want to be God and control the future rather than have to trust God and follow him as he leads us into it prove we're not God also.

It seems that Belshazzar wouldn't have thought to consider any of this in response to those questions either. He wouldn't have cared to even consider how God would feel about any of it.

I'm sure you've considered what God thinks. I'm certain of it, actually. You wouldn't be reading a book like this if that weren't the case. Even if you didn't think of yourself *first* as something that's regularly getting in the way of your most satisfying existence, you likely picked up a book like this, a book about God, because some combination of your past, present, and future proves something about you that's sometimes hard to live with.

You aren't God. Because you're not God, you need God. You need God's help.

But while God used some strange words written by a strange floating hand to tell Belshazzar that he wasn't going to receive God's help on account of his pride, there's another strange word in the Bible that assures us that we have it. And we never have to doubt it. That word is *Jeshurun*.

Moses used this word in Deuteronomy chapter 33. It was at the end of Israel's 40-year journey in the wilderness toward the Promised Land. The past 40 years had been filled with tremendous pain. In the present, they were alive but living with a great deal of regret and loss. It was true for every person entering their new home—none of their parents were still living. Even Moses, their great God-given deliverer, wasn't going to enter into the land with them. While the future in the Promised Land certainly sounded promising, it was still the future. As such, it was a bit uncertain, especially with some very unfriendly nations still occupying the land God had promised them.

Moses had one last opportunity to calm God's people. During his farewell speech, as part of the final words Moses spoke while on earth, he assured them that **"there is no one like the God of Jeshurun, who rides across the heavens to help you"** (Deuteronomy 33:26).

To help illustrate what the word *Jeshurun* means, I'm going to tell you about Kelsey. Kelsey became very sick when she was nearly nine months pregnant. She slipped into a coma because of it. While she was in her coma, she gave birth to a beautiful and healthy baby girl named Lucy, but Kelsey remained in her coma for the next ten weeks, needing a double lung transplant in order to live, the doctors said.

She hadn't received that lung transplant yet when she suddenly woke up from her coma after ten weeks and was no longer in need of a lung transplant to keep living. She was completely healthy, and she continued to be. She was better.

Now I want you to think about the moment Kelsey woke up and was told she had given birth to a healthy girl ten weeks earlier. In particular, I want you to think about how

Kelsey would have felt when she saw her little daughter for the first time. *That* feeling gets us close to the meaning of the word *Jeshurun*.

Jeshurun was Israel's poetic name, one intended to communicate a feeling of impossible-to-describe-fully delight in how God viewed his people. It means God saw them only and always in the best and most beautiful way. No flaws. No reason to push them away ever. That's how Kelsey looked at Lucy after her coma. And it's how God always looks at you now after what Jesus accomplished on the cross, where your past was forgiven, your future with Jesus in perfection was guaranteed, and God showed how determined he really is to stay by your side in every present moment.

Consider that again:

- *Your past is forgiven.* **"There is now no condemnation for those who are in Christ Jesus"** (Romans 8:1).
- *God is with you in the present.* **"Always, to the very end"** (Matthew 28:20).
- *Your perfect future with Jesus is guaranteed.* It's where **"God will wipe away every tear from their eyes"** (Revelation 7:17).

You don't even need to be God or even see how God is working in order for that to happen. You only need to be where you are right now: safe in the arms of your Savior who rules over all time for your benefit.

GOD UNDERSTANDS YOUR LEGACY

Review Daniel 5:25-29.

Real Life

Jackson was excited to attend college on a full-ride football scholarship. He would be the first in his family to attend college. The summer before his first semester, however, he was involved in a major car accident. The damage sustained to his legs meant his football days were done, and he lost his scholarship. He was crushed. He had no idea what his future was going to look like. He believed that everything he had lived for was now a waste.

1. How would you encourage Jackson in his situation? Would you point him more to the past, the present, or the future?

2. How might you use Belshazzar's experience to help Jackson gain a good perspective?

Questions

1. In what ways does our world "weigh and measure" success differently from God's standards?

2. The writing on the wall points to the ultimate judgment we all face—that of being judged by God. But because Jesus bore the weight of our sins, securing our eternity with him, that's a judgment we don't need to fear. Do

you still sometimes feel afraid of God's judgment over your life? If so, why? If not, why not?

3. Which of the following do you think Christians have the most difficult time with:

   When they carry heavy regrets from their past

   When their present circumstances are unbearable

   When they can't see a good way forward to a better future

4. Imagine God came to you and said your time on earth will end in exactly 28 days. What would you immediately start doing, stop doing, or keep doing in your life?

GOD UNDERSTANDS YOUR LEGACY

DAY 19: YOU'LL NEVER KNOW WHEN

Open Your Bible
Read Daniel 5:30,31.

A dangerous tropical storm was forecasted to make its way through the state of Florida. Flights in and out of the state were canceled. Residents tried to drive far away from it before it arrived, but not everyone could.

A 32-year-old woman named Heather lived in a mobile home. As the winds began to increase dramatically, she planned to shelter at home and wait out the storm. But the storm didn't cooperate. A tornado ripped through her mobile home, picked her up, threw her 200 feet, and killed her. She didn't know that was going to happen that day. Yet it still did, and she wasn't able to stop it from happening.

King Belshazzar had a similar experience after Daniel interpreted the handwriting on the wall for him. The last two verses of Daniel chapter 5 say very simply, **"That very night Belshazzar, king of the Babylonians, was slain, and Darius the Mede took over the kingdom, at the age of sixty-two"** (verses 30,31). Belshazzar's life was over just like that. When he woke up that morning, he didn't know it was going to happen that day. Yet it still did, and he wasn't able to stop it from happening.

While tornadoes and strange fingers suddenly appearing in the middle of a dinner party and etching some graffiti on the wall aren't common occurrences to many, surprising reminders of how short life is or can be are all around us.

Just this morning before I started writing, news broke that a helicopter collided with a commercial airplane full of passengers. Many died. Hearts are broken. If anyone boarding that airplane knew it was going to happen, they wouldn't have gotten on. If anyone whose spouse, child, parent, or friend was getting on that plane had known this was going to happen, they never would have allowed them to leave home this morning. But they didn't know, just like we don't. We don't know when deadly sickness will strike. We don't know when an accident at work will happen. We don't know when a person will be at the wrong place at the wrong time. We don't know when someone else's night of too much drinking will collide with the fragile life of someone we love. We don't know. It's why we often feel afraid.

The same was true of Jesus' disciples. In Mark chapter 4, they were afraid in the middle of a storm. They weren't unfamiliar with the water. A number of them made their living as fishermen. They were experienced with the winds and the waves, but that day as the powerful waves crashed again and again against their fragile boat, leading them to believe that they were all going to drown, they realized the same thing Heather in Florida did. You can't just stop a storm. Unless . . .

Unless your voice is the same one that spoke the universe into existence and drove out demons and laid the earth's foundations and marked off its dimensions. It's the voice of the guy who was sleeping comfortably in the same boat in which those disciples were drowning.

"Why are you so afraid?" Jesus asked his disciples after they woke him from his nap; after they questioned the depth of his care for them; and after he got up, rebuked the wind, told the waves to **"be still!"** and everything was still. All was calm. (See Mark 4:35-41.)

Why were they afraid? Maybe because they couldn't make that happen. Maybe because they had doubted Jesus. Maybe because they wondered what someone who was clearly capable of *anything* might do to those who doubt the depth of his care for them. But they didn't need to fear that. "Why are you so afraid?" Jesus asked his disciples after they had just seen what we clearly see from over two thousand years away—that what he's capable of doing to anyone who doubts him . . . is saving them. He's capable of calming the storm for them, and he's not only capable. He's willing. He's not just willing to help. Remember where he was the whole time. He was right in the boat with them. He was already exactly where his vulnerable friends needed him to be when the storm they could neither avoid nor control came rushing toward them.

Heather wasn't alone either on that tornado day. When she ran into her mobile home, she cradled in her arms her three-year-old daughter, AnneMarie, determined not to let her go no matter what happened. And she didn't let her go.

Heather had her cradled in her arms the whole time, even when she was lifted 200 feet into the air by the winds of that tornado. Heather held her daughter so tightly and securely that when the rescue squad came through after the storm was done and found both mother and daughter together, AnneMarie was still breathing. She survived her storm. Why? Because she was loved by someone.

You are loved by the God who is capable of silencing every storm. He chose to hang on a cross in the middle of a pitch-dark sky and do nothing except use all his strength to hold you in the safe place of his promised redemption. He did it so the one thing you could know as you make your way through this world's sudden and overwhelming storms, struggles, and temptations is that asking if Jesus cares about you is a foolish question.

At the cross you have a Friend who is both able and willing to save you. He's a Friend who is already exactly where you need him to be when the storms of sin and death come rushing toward you. The only thing you need to do to survive every one of them is nothing. Be still.

You may not know when your earthly end is coming, but you do know what happens after it does. **"Do not let your hearts be troubled,"** Jesus told his disciples on the night before he was crucified. **"My Father's house has many rooms. . . . I am going there to prepare a place for you"** (John 14:1,2).

For *you*.

GOD UNDERSTANDS YOUR LEGACY

Review Daniel 5:30,31.

Real Life

Ethan's best friend Eric died after a short but intense battle with cancer. Ethan was crushed. At the funeral, Eric's mother told Ethan that Eric had left something for him. Eric wanted Ethan to have his Bible, the one in which Eric had written all his prayers and observations about Scripture. Every page was full of Eric's writing.

1. What do you think was most meaningful about that for Ethan?

   The gift of the Bible itself

   That Eric trusted Ethan with his personal thoughts

   That Eric was thinking of Ethan leading up to his death, wanting to do something meaningful for him

2. What do you think Eric's gift taught Ethan about death for Christians?

Questions

1. What did Belshazzar's feast reveal about his attitude toward God? Where do you see similar attitudes toward God in the world today?

2. Why do you think Belshazzar honored Daniel even after hearing the bad news?

GOD UNDERSTANDS

3. What would you like people to remember about you when your life on earth is done?

4. What can you do differently in your life right now to help you accomplish your answer(s) to the previous question.

GOD UNDERSTANDS YOUR LIONS

—

Daniel Chapter 6

DAY 20: JEALOUSY

Open Your Bible
Read Daniel 6:1-5.

In the late 1890s, Lieutenant Colonel John Henry Patterson was ordered to oversee the building of a railway bridge over the Tsavo River in Kenya. One morning shortly after his arrival, Lieutenant Colonel Patterson woke up and discovered that a handful of his workers had been attacked by lions overnight. The lions had crept into the camp while the workers were sleeping, dragged the men out of their tents, and killed them.

This spooked the remaining workers, who then decided to build thorn barriers around the camp to keep the lions out. It didn't work. The lions crawled through the thorns, dragged their new victims out, and killed them too.

The remaining workers lit bonfires at night and set what they thought were safe curfews for everyone. It didn't work. The lions continued to get in and take new victims.

It was later discovered that there were only two lions doing all this damage, but each of them was over 9 feet long. Between the two of them, they eventually dragged away dozens of victims.

The lions became known as the Tsavo Man-Eaters. Many of Lieutenant Colonel Patterson's workers left the project because they were scared for their lives. Patterson, however, never left. He decided to hunt the lions. After many weeks, he successfully killed one. Two weeks later, he killed the other. He made their skins into rugs that covered the floor of his den until 1924 when he sold them to the Field Museum in Chicago, where they are currently on display. Today, these ferocious beasts can hurt you exactly as much as Daniel's lions hurt him.

We are now in Daniel chapter 6, which is easily the most well-known and treasured portion of this book—the famous account of Daniel in the lions' den. Daniel was between 80 and 90 years old at this time, and life was going well for him. Chapter 6 introduces us to the third king under whom Daniel served—a man named Darius, who took over the same night King Belshazzar was struck down by God in the year 539 B.C. Through his faithful service to multiple kings and through his faithful service to God over many decades, Daniel had now established himself as a reliable, productive, and faithful citizen. We get the impression from this chapter that Darius liked Daniel immensely.

So how did Daniel, so well-liked by King Darius, end up in the den of Darius' lions? By the attack of a different type of lion. One without teeth yet still capable of ripping a person's heart to shreds. One without muscles yet still capable of destroying lives in an instant. This lion, if you were to call it that, can be just as much a threat to a person's soul as the

Tsavo Man-Eaters were to Lieutenant Colonel Patterson's workers in Kenya.

This lion is jealousy. You may never be face-to-face with wild lions, but you will have to find a way to deal with jealousy. Daniel did. Jealousy is the reason the den of lions even became a possibility for him. Daniel wasn't jealous. That wasn't the problem. Others were jealous of him.

King Darius wasn't from Babylon, as the two previous kings Daniel served had been—Nebuchadnezzar and Belshazzar. Darius was from Persia. Babylon, a dominant world power under Nebuchadnezzar, had become weak and vulnerable under the poor leadership of his son Belshazzar. Persia pounced on those weaknesses the night Belshazzar died, and Darius immediately took over. Just as it happens in the transition from one American president to the next when there are many new faces brought in with the new regime to take over roles previously occupied by different people, the same thing happened here. Darius brought in a new leadership team, new advisors, and new people to oversee the new government. Somehow Daniel made the cut of those from the previous government who were allowed to keep serving. Actually, he more than made the cut. Darius made Daniel one of three administrators tasked with overseeing the entire kingdom. At the beginning of this chapter, we're told that Darius was planning to make Daniel the one person responsible for overseeing the whole kingdom. But we also learn that not everyone was happy for Daniel.

It's not that they disliked him as a person or thought he

didn't deserve the position. **"They could find no corruption in him,"** we're told, **"because he was trustworthy and neither corrupt nor negligent"** (verse 4). They just disliked what Daniel had *in comparison to themselves.*

Their lives weren't bad at all. In a nation estimated to have a population of around 200,000, this group that was conspiring against Daniel was among the 120 most powerful of those citizens. They had already received and enjoyed ranks of positions, authority, benefits, and trust that 99.94% of their neighbors never would. They weren't lacking.

They only lacked *in comparison to Daniel.* Daniel had a position that they didn't have. Daniel had authority that they hadn't been given. Daniel received benefits they didn't get to enjoy. Daniel had a level of the king's trust that they hadn't yet earned.

Maybe if they kept working hard and proving their faithfulness and competence for the tasks like Daniel had over many decades, they would eventually have an opportunity to earn that place for themselves. Daniel, as an aged man by this point, certainly wasn't going to serve in his position for long. They could have waited until his retirement, but they didn't want to wait, and they didn't want to work for it. They wanted what Daniel had, they wanted it immediately, and they weren't going to be happy—with themselves or anyone else—until they had it.

They were jealous. In their jealousy, they plotted to remove Daniel from his position as quickly as possible. Their plan was to approach the king and trick him into establishing a law they knew would trap Daniel. We'll talk more about that in upcoming days. But for now, it's important to know that jealousy wasn't just a problem in Daniel's world.

It can happen today anytime someone opens up social media, looks at any of the countless lives so perfectly portrayed there, and asks themselves, "How do I compare?" Or when someone looks at a neighbor whose quality of house, car, income, spouse, children, or ease of life are seemingly better than theirs. Or when someone sizes themselves up against someone younger, prettier, curvier, smoother, or well-liked than they are. Or in countless other ways when they might be tempted to dislike where they are, what they have, or who they are in comparison to someone else.

There's nothing wrong with noticing differences. The difference between Daniel's position and those of the 120 others was obvious, just as obvious as the fact that Darius was the king and Daniel wasn't. Noticing the differences only becomes dangerous when it's used as a reason to be discontent with ourselves or to damage anyone else. Whenever that discontentment happens, I would venture to say that what the discontented person is trying hard to make true about themselves is something God has already declared to be true through Jesus.

> You are God's chosen royalty. (1 Peter 2:9)
>
> You are God's work of art. (Ephesians 2:10)
>
> You are God's advisor. (1 John 5:14,15)

You are loved. (1 John 4:9)

You are strong. (2 Corinthians 12:9)

You are noticed and understood. (Psalm 139:1,2)

You are God's unique gift to this world. (1 Corinthians 12:4-7)

And in case it's easy for you to recall times when you have acted in ways that are contrary to who God says you are . . . You are forgiven. (Psalm 103:12)

These are all things that you already are through Jesus because of his work, because of his life, because of his sacrifice. You don't have to work for them. You don't have to earn them. You certainly don't have to conspire to hurt anyone in order to enjoy them. That's what Daniel's peers were attempting to do. That was jealousy. That was wrong. That was sin. **"You have been set free from sin"** (Romans 6:18).

Wherever you are in life, whatever the details of your life (or anyone else's) look like, there's no need to let jealousy live in your heart one moment longer. Not when you know who you are to God.

Review Daniel 6:1-5.

Real Life

Stacey was on a full-ride track scholarship to her college. Continuing to receive the scholarship was dependent on both her performance on the track as well as in the classroom. She needed to perform well. As a result, she studied and trained a lot. One night during a study break, she checked her social media and saw pictures of her friends hanging out downtown and laughing together. She felt sad that she wasn't with them and wanted to quit, not just at track and school. She wanted her life to be over.

1. Do you think Stacey's reaction to what she saw on social media is a common or uncommon reaction in today's world? Explain your answer.

2. What comparisons do you see Stacey making?

3. If you were Stacey's roommate, what might you do or say when you notice she's feeling down about her life?

Questions

Read through each of the passages referenced in this chapter regarding who God says you are and discuss the following two questions:

1. Which one is the most difficult for you to believe? Why do you think you chose the one you did?

2. Which is your favorite at this point in your life? Explain your answer.

Here are the passages:

   1 Peter 2:9

   Ephesians 2:10

   1 John 5:14,15

   1 John 4:9

   2 Corinthians 12:9

   Psalm 139:1,2

   1 Corinthians 12:4-7

   Psalm 103:12

   Romans 6:18

DAY 21: PRIDE

Open Your Bible
Read Daniel 6:6–16.

Nebuchadnezzar was the first king under whom Daniel served. God sent Nebuchadnezzar two troubling dreams to warn him about his pride. At one point, God took away Nebuchadnezzar's power and made his existence into that of a strange animal—until he repented of his pride. He eventually did, and both his humanity and his power were given back to him.

Belshazzar was the second king under whom Daniel served. During a party one evening, God made a hand appear, and the hand wrote a message on a wall. The message wasn't just a warning against Belshazzar's personal pride. It was a declaration that God had already judged his prideful heart. God ended his life that evening.

Darius was the third king under whom Daniel served. He wasn't from Babylon. He was from Persia, so maybe you couldn't blame him if he didn't know *everything* about the lives of the kings who had preceded him. But you might think that those who had witnessed a hand appear out of nowhere and write a cryptic message on a wall or a king acting like a bird—two clear lessons from Daniel's God on the dangers of pride—might be inclined to tell the new guy he should stay far away from pride. Maybe they did. Maybe Daniel even did. Yet for the third time, Daniel found himself living in the very dangerous place of a king's pride-filled existence.

When the group that was jealous of Daniel came to Darius and suggested that everyone in his kingdom should pray to him alone for the next 30 days with the promise that anyone who wouldn't would be thrown into a den of lions, for whatever reason, Darius agreed. But part of the reason a person agrees to be worshiped must be because they, in some part of their heart, believe they are worthy of it. It doesn't seem Darius thought little of himself.

We also know Darius thought very highly of Daniel. Yet by the end of the day on which Darius was going to make him the most trusted and powerful man underneath him, Darius would have Daniel thrown into a den of lions. We know Darius did not at all want that to happen. So how did it? How did the one person in the whole kingdom who may have loved Daniel the most become the one who made the rule that would seemingly kill Daniel? Easy. It happened accidentally. That's how pride works. It works very subtly and is often only recognized in a person's life long after it has done its damage.

Just look at another well-known example of pride in the Bible. To Jesus' other disciples, this man had a great reputation. Jesus called him to be a disciple after all, just like them. He willingly left his previous life, whatever that was, and decided to follow Jesus, knowing already from the beginning that there was no health insurance and no pension. He went on various mission trips to preach the gospel, sometimes with the 12, at least one time with 72 followers of Jesus. Jesus himself included this disciple in everything—even washing his feet and serving him Lord's Supper on Maundy Thursday. That's what the disciples knew about Judas.

Even as he was on his way out the door to take the final step in betraying Jesus—after Jesus had told them that *one of them* would betray him, after he said it was the one who would dip his hand into the bowl with him, and after Judas dipped his hand into the bowl with Jesus—the disciples assumed Judas was leaving to tidy up some financial preparations. They never suspected him. Which means that after they saw Judas hand Jesus over to his enemies and later that same night heard the shocking news that Judas had died from hanging, I think it's likely that many of the disciples asked the very understandable question, "How did this happen?"

We still ask that question today. We ask it when the life of someone we know takes a turn in an unexpected direction. We ask it when we see our society doing unspeakable things that inflict unspeakable pain and carrying on as if they don't even care that it's happening. Like the disciples, we sometimes even ask that question when we think of people we went to church with.

Some years back, I had driven to my church in the middle of the afternoon. I was parking my car on the street outside the church entrance when I saw a woman walking down the sidewalk. As I turned off my car, another car swerved in front of me, its back door was thrown open, the woman jumped in, and they drove away. There were two men in the front seat. Do you know what they had just done? They had just picked up a prostitute, but not just any prostitute. This particular woman grew up attending Christian schools, was in church with both her parents and all her siblings every weekend, and had family in the church I was currently pastoring. How does something like that happen? The same way it always does. The same way it did for Judas. Accidentally.

Judas never wanted to become and never thought he would become someone whom no parent would want to name a child after. Someone who would end up turning the Savior over to his betrayers. Someone who would himself betray "innocent blood," as Judas himself eventually said. Yet he did. How?

The Bible gives us information about Judas that his fellow disciples didn't know. In John chapter 12, a woman anointed Jesus' feet with expensive perfume, and Judas got upset, pointing out that the money could have been used for so many other things, like feeding the poor. The disciples apparently didn't disagree when they heard him say that, but God wanted us to know what was going on in his heart when he did. **"He did not say this because he cared about the poor but because he was a thief; as keeper of the money bag, he used to help himself to what was put into it"** (John 12:6). That is something the other disciples didn't know about him. They didn't know that Judas had a greedy heart.

It wasn't the sin of greed that hurt Judas in the end. Greed is one of countless sins for which Jesus earned forgiveness. It was failing to repent of it. It was Judas thinking that someone like him wasn't really vulnerable to being destroyed by greed. That's pride.

Pride isn't just feeling self-important, like Darius. It's finding your safest place and warmest comfort in your self-importance. That will always leave a person blind to what's really happening to them. Jesus saw it in Judas, however: **"Very truly I tell you, one of you is going to betray me,"** he said just hours before it happened (John 13:21). And in the phrase immediately before Jesus said those words, the Bible lets us know how Jesus was feeling when he said it: **"Jesus was troubled in spirit."** Jesus knew what was going on in Judas' heart, and it troubled him.

What do you think troubles him when he looks at our world, the one in which you and I live? As he looks into all our hearts, whom would he identify as someone who is continuing to indulge in something they know is sin? It doesn't have to be greed. It could be jealousy. Resentment. Lust. Drunkenness. Arrogance. Self-centeredness. What would Jesus see in your heart if he were right next to you today? Because that's where Judas was sitting during the Passover meal on Maundy Thursday. From what we know about seating arrangements in Jesus' day and using the detail the Bible gives us, we know the disciple John was sitting at Jesus' right, and it seems clear that Jesus placed Judas immediately to his left, in the seat typically reserved for the host's closest friend. Judas and Jesus sat so close that they shared everything. They shared the bowl into which they dipped their bread. They heard every syllable the other person said. Judas heard Jesus say, "One of you will betray me." He would have seen the lump in Jesus' throat when he said, **"What you are about to do, do quickly"** (John 13:27).

It was only after Judas did hand Jesus over to his enemies, after he received his money, and only after he saw the immense pain his seemingly insignificant sin of unrepented greed inflicted on a man who had only always been good to him that he realized what big damage a little sin like pride or greed is capable of doing. And it broke him. Then he believed in the seriousness of breaking any part of God's law and was determined never to do anything like it again. **"I have betrayed innocent blood,"** he confessed (Matthew 27:4). He *confessed* his sin. But if you think that means Judas was saved from his pride, you are wrong. Because after seeing his sin and confessing it, there's one thing he didn't see. He didn't see something I saw some years ago on a snowy Sunday morning.

The snow started heavy on Saturday evening, and it was still going strong Sunday morning. This was before the days of live streaming much of anything, which meant that if church was cancelled, it wasn't happening. I woke up early and made my way to church to evaluate the conditions. The heavy falling snow was pushing hard against the car in 40 mph winds. The roads hadn't been plowed. I drove by an SUV that had wrapped itself around a light post. My standard for canceling things at church had been to ask if I would feel okay having my kids on the roads in those conditions. And I didn't. So I cancelled church. We put the announcement on the news. I called everyone I could think of to tell them but decided to stay there throughout the morning in case someone happened to show up. Eventually, one person did.

I was surprised by who it was. I hadn't seen her in church in months. In fact, the last time I had seen her she was outside of church, getting into the back of a car with two young men. She was the prostitute. She didn't have a phone or television or an internet connection to tell her not to come in. As horrible as the driving conditions were that morning, it was worse walking. But she did. She forced her way through high-intensity winds, was completely covered with snow when she walked in, and when I told her church was canceled, said, "But this is the only place I wanted to be this morning." Why? Because she believed something Judas apparently never did. She believed the gospel; she believed that there really is good news for someone whose heart is so deeply broken with sin. She believed that when Jesus was surrounded by soldiers in the Garden of Gethsemane and looked into the eyes of the man who led them there, whose heart he had clearly seen from the very beginning, and called him his friend, he meant it. He meant it so much so that he still washed Judas' feet that night and served him the Lord's Supper, the very body and blood he would offer on a cross less than a day later to forgive him. He meant it so much so that he was willing to struggle under the weight of a heavy cross while being assaulted by the high-intensity winds of the whole world's sins just so every hurting and guilty soul who stumbles their way through the snow could find hope and a reason to start all over again.

Judas didn't see it that way. When he confessed his sin, he didn't fall at the feet of the innocent man walking to a cross to be punished instead of him. He confessed to the people who hired him to indulge it, and then he went out and died believing one very destructive lie also rooted in pride that is focused far more on self than on anything Jesus did: that there isn't room in our Father's house for someone as guilty as him.

There would have been room. That's what the woman at church saw on that snowy morning. She saw the truth, that no matter how far you've strayed, no matter how deep your pride, no matter how dark your sin, you have a Friend who knows your whole heart, who believes with his whole heart that it is forgiven, and who wants you to believe the good news that the one place you will always belong is in the place that is right next to him in our Father's house. Every step of the way there, we walk with him.

First Peter 5:8 reminds us that our **"enemy the devil prowls around like a roaring lion looking for someone to devour."** We might describe pride in the same way, which would be fitting since it seems that pride was Satan's original sin that took him from the perfection of God's presence to the hell of eternal suffering.

Daniel had to deal with sins of pride under each of three kings in such profound and difficult ways. It's in some ways a reminder that pride will always be an enemy we must be ready to face—in ourselves just as much as in anyone else.

But the account of Darius gives us hope. Though Darius indulged his pride, that doesn't mean it ended up owning him. We see a glimpse of that in what Darius said to Daniel as Daniel was being thrown in front of the lions. **"May your God, whom you serve continually, rescue you!"** (verse 16). In that sentence, Darius mentioned Daniel's God. Darius mentioned Daniel. Darius mentioned Daniel's obvious allegiance to God, but Darius didn't mention Darius at all. How did that happen?

At this point in Daniel chapter 6, God is just getting ready to teach Darius and us the power and grace of the God Daniel was clearly serving.

Review Daniel 6:6–16.

Real Life

Lindsey attended a high school where she was among the minority as a Christian. Her classmates were openly critical of her Christian faith on a regular basis. Leading up to a big school dance one year, her classmates conspired to play a trick on Lindsey. One of the most popular boys in the school asked Lindsey to go to the dance with him; he asked her in a very public way that got a lot of attention. Once she said yes, he immediately took back the invitation, harshly criticized her religion, and made fun of her for thinking she belonged with someone like him.

1. What details about the life of Daniel might you share with Lindsey to encourage her.

2. Hebrews 4:15 tells us that when Jesus lived on earth, he was **"tempted in every way, just as we are."** What moments in the life of Jesus might you point Lindsey toward to remind her that Jesus knows how she feels?

Questions

1. Pride was very much in the hearts of each of the three kings under whom Daniel served. Do you think that's because of the leadership positions they held or because they were human? Explain your answer.

2. Can you think of examples in your life or anyone else's where pride led to a painful downfall or to repentance?

3. After the decree had been published, Daniel both thanked God and asked God for help in his next prayer.

   For what do you think Daniel thanked God?

   In what way do you think Daniel asked for help?

   Do you think God answered Daniel's prayer for help in the way Daniel was expecting? Why or why not?

DAY 22: FEAR

Open Your Bible
Read Daniel 6:17–28

In June 2023, an airplane carrying three adults and four children crashed in the Colombian Amazon Rainforest. The area in which the plane crashed was so dense and difficult to get to that it took 16 days for rescuers to arrive at the crash site. When they finally did, the rescue team found the bodies of all three adults who had been on the airplane. They were dead. But the bodies of the four children were nowhere to be found.

A search for the children—ages 13, 9, 4, and a newborn—began in earnest. About 150 soldiers and dogs were flown into the area to team up with dozens of volunteers who had joined in. Finally, 40 days after the crash, the children were found. They were all alive. They had all survived not only a plane crash but also nearly a month and a half on their own in a very dangerous jungle.

How did they do that?

It seems they had a couple of very important things with them. First, they knew to take a mosquito net with them as they left the plane. It was important for keeping deadly bugs away while they were sleeping. Second, they took food with them from the airplane and were wise about not eating it all at once. Additionally, the older children had some knowledge about how to find suitable food in the jungle. Third, they grabbed and carried with them the entire 40 days an 11-pound bag of flour. When the baby was hungry, they mixed some of the flour with water from the jungle to create a very basic form of baby food. Finally, and most important, they had courage.

Having courage doesn't mean you aren't afraid. Courage is the willingness to take a single step forward when you don't know how it's going to go. That's what those children did. That's what they kept doing: single step after single step for 40 days. They had courage.

That's what Daniel did as he walked into the den of lions. Make no mistake—Daniel did not know how this was going to go. Or maybe he did. After all, he was an aged, edible human about to be served up on a platter designed for hungry lions. Even the king, the one man in the best position to help, had his hands tied by the irrevocable and unchangeable **"law of the Medes and Persians"** (verse 15).

"A stone was brought and placed over the mouth of the den, and the king sealed it with his own signet ring and with the rings of his nobles, so that Daniel's situation might not be changed" (verse 17).

Not a word from Daniel is recorded through any of this. What was he thinking? What was he expecting would happen? What was he praying? Was he afraid? A lot? A little bit?

Was he hoping it would end quickly? We don't know. We are not told. But single step by single step he walked into the den as all of this happened. That's how we know he had courage. We also know how he got himself into a position where he would need it. He was living by faith.

At the end of the ordeal, after Daniel survived a full night in the den of lions, we're told that **"when Daniel was lifted from the den, no wound was found on him, because he had trusted in his God"** (verse 23). He trusted in God.

What exactly was he thinking about God as he trusted in him? Maybe he was thinking of a verse in the Bible like this one: **"'For I know the plans I have for you,' declares the Lord, 'plans to prosper you and not to harm you, plans to give you hope and a future.'"**

You may recognize that as Jeremiah 29:11, a favorite of many Christians because it serves as a reminder of God's loving involvement in every part of our lives. It's an encouraging assurance that whatever our present happens to be, however difficult or troubling, it will not keep God from carrying out his good future plans for us. To many, this verse is a God-given reason to keep going, single step by single step, because it contains a promise that better days are coming. Prosperous days.

Daniel recognized this verse too. It was in a letter that had been sent to Babylon from the prophet Jeremiah while Daniel was serving under Nebuchadnezzar. Jeremiah and Daniel were contemporaries. While Daniel was taken from Judah when the Babylonians first conquered Jerusalem,

Jeremiah remained behind to minister to the others who were left there.

In Jeremiah chapter 29, we are given the text of a letter Jeremiah sent to Daniel and the other exiles while they were away. This verse was in it. But if Daniel and his friends took that verse as a promise from God that they were soon returning home, they were mistaken. The verse immediately before that one said something quite different: **"This is what the Lord says: 'When seventy years are completed for Babylon, I will come to you and fulfill my good promise to bring you back to this place'"** (verse 10). 70 years? That meant Daniel was likely never going home.

Which is why Jeremiah gave this advice earlier in the letter: **"Build houses and settle down; plant gardens and eat what they produce. Marry and have sons and daughters; find wives for your sons and give your daughters in marriage, so that they too may have sons and daughters. Increase in number there; do not decrease. Also, seek the peace and prosperity of the city to which I have carried you into exile. Pray to the Lord for it, because if it prospers, you too will prosper"** (verses 5-7).

In other words, "Settle into your new home in Babylon, friends. Establish your life and family as well as you can, remembering that, 'I know the plans I have for you,' declares the Lord, 'plans to prosper you and not to harm you, plans to give you hope and future.' God won't forget about you. So don't forget about him."

Daniel obviously didn't. He practiced his faith faithfully.

So faithfully, in fact, that **"when Daniel learned that the decree had been published, he went home to his upstairs room where the windows opened toward Jerusalem. Three times a day he got down on his knees and prayed, giving thanks to his God, just as he had done before"** (Daniel 6:10).

"Just as he had done before." That's important. Some might ask why Daniel didn't just close the window during his prayer time to spare himself some possible discomfort or pain? Because then a threat to his faith would have been the reason he stopped practicing it the way he normally did. He would have shown himself as someone who was more afraid of a threat than he was confident in the God he already served. And if a threat to your faith can change how you practice it, or whether or not you're willing to practice it at all, then someone might rightly ask—Was it really faith to begin with, or were you just doing something that seemed good and didn't cost much of anything? Daniel's faith cost him something.

That may never happen to you in exactly the same way that it happened to Daniel. You may never be in a position where you have to decide to step closer to a lion or further away, but you may have to choose between keeping your job or leaving it without any benefits if you're ordered to be dishonest in your recordkeeping or to help carry out an abortion. You may have to choose between keeping your friends or taking your next steps without them if they're urging you to get drunk alongside them one evening. Or maybe it's not an external threat that's challenging your faith. It's the pull of a familiar temptation, along with the lie that you'll be better off if you give in. It's the false promise that you'll be better off if you walk away from your unhappy marriage, even though you know your reasons for wanting to do so are not biblically legitimate.

That's not to say these situations are easy. It wasn't easy for Daniel to walk toward a den of lions. It wasn't easy for Jesus when his own church called for his crucifixion or when the government he appointed and empowered made it happen. It wasn't easy to be hung high on a cross, to look out at the faces of those who had spit upon him and say, "Father, forgive them." It wasn't easy for the holy Son of God to leave heaven, to be born in human flesh as a baby, and to walk single step by single step toward a sacrifice his Father had promised was coming. It wasn't easy to die—and then rise to life again. But he did it because he wanted to give you something reliable to put your faith in whenever you're afraid or far from home or guilty or vulnerable or standing all alone.

He wanted to give you God. A gracious God (Ephesians 2:8,9). A loving God (1 John 4:10). A powerful God (Matthew 19:26). A forgiving God (Luke 15:11-32). A God who has great plans for you and will not allow any den, any lion, any enemy, anyone else's pride, and not even any of the times your fear has overwhelmed your faith to stop his plans from happening (Jeremiah 29:11).

Sure, Daniel likely would have preferred to avoid any situation that would require courage. No doubt you would too. But Jesus knows the type of world in which you're living. It's one in which courage is needed on account of everything that can make you feel afraid. Remember that he lived here too. He sees you. When the world sees you living with courage—Christian courage—then as Darius did when Daniel came walking out of the lions' den, an unbelieving world might just see the greatness of your God too. They may never see it without you or your life of faith.

Single step by single step, you can keep going. Daniel did. Notice one more thing that happened because he did. In particular, I want you to notice one specific word God included in the very last verse of this section. Here's the verse: **"So Daniel prospered during the reign of Darius and the reign of Cyrus the Persian"** (verse 28).

Did you notice the word? *Prospered.* "So Daniel prospered," just like God promised he would in Jeremiah 29:11: **"'I know the plans I have for you,' declares the Lord, 'plans to prosper you and not to harm you, plans to give you hope and a future.'"**

God didn't forget. He hasn't forgotten you either. He knows. It's going to be OK.

Review Daniel 6:17-28.

Real Life

Anthony was a construction manager who became a Christian as an adult. When his church organized a mission trip to another country to help build an orphanage, looking specifically for people with building skills, he was excited to go and help, even though he knew the country was openly hostile to Christians. While they were there, their camp was overtaken by a group of government soldiers. Anthony was arrested, placed in prison, and told that he would only be released to return home if he denounced his Christian faith and promised never to return.

1. If you were in Anthony's position, what would you consider to be a successful outcome in this situation?

2. Imagine that Anthony's wife and children are not Christian. How do you think Anthony would best serve them in this situation?

Questions

1. God didn't keep Daniel from the den of lions, though he had the power to do so. Rather, he allowed Daniel to face the lions, in part, it seems, because God wanted to use Daniel's faithfulness to impact the heart of Darius positively. What lessons might you learn from Daniel regarding how God uses his people to impact an unbelieving world?

2. Read the following Bible passages mentioned earlier in this section. Take note of what they each tell you about

God. Then pick the one that means the most to you at this point in your life and explain why you chose it:

Ephesians 2:8,9

1 John 4:10

Matthew 19:26

Luke 15:11–32

3. What similarities do you see between Daniel's situation in the den of lions and Jesus' trial, death, and resurrection? How are those situations different?

4. Where do you think Christian courage is especially needed in the world today?

NOTES

1. "Incidence of Neonatal Abstinence Syndrome—28 States, 1999–2013," *Morbidity and Mortality Weekly Report*, CDC, August 12, 2016, https://www.cdc.gov/mmwr/volumes/65/wr/mm6531a2.htm.

2. "Domestic Violence Statistics," National Domestic Violence Hotline, https://www.thehotline.org/stakeholders/domestic-violence-statistics/ and "Suicide Data and Statistics," Suicide Prevention, CDC, https://www.cdc.gov/suicide/facts/data.html.

ABOUT THE AUTHOR

Pastor Jeremy Mattek currently serves at a growing mission church in Conroe, Texas. He is also a regular contributor to Time of Grace video and written content and the creator of the video/podcast series Bible Breath and the popular Evening Encouragements devotions.

ABOUT TIME OF GRACE

The mission of Time of Grace is to point people to what matters most: Jesus. Using a variety of media (television, radio, podcasts, print publications, and digital), Time of Grace teaches tough topics in an approachable and relatable way, accessible in multiple languages, making the Bible clear and understandable for those who need encouragement in their walks of faith and for those who don't yet know Jesus at all.

To discover more, please visit timeofgrace.org or scan this code:

HELP SHARE GOD'S MESSAGE OF GRACE!

Every gift you give helps Time of Grace reach people around the world with the good news of Jesus. Your generosity and prayer support take the gospel of grace to others through our ministry outreach and help them experience a satisfied life as they see God all around them.

Give today at timeofgrace.org/give, by calling 800.661.3311, or by scanning the code below.

Thank you!